TOOLKIT ON MAPPING LEGAL, HEALTH AND SOCIAL SERVICES RESPONSES TO CHILD MALTREATMENT

World Health Organization

Lucerne University of
Applied Sciences and Arts

HOCHSCHULE
LUZERN

Social Work
FH Zentralschweiz

CRIMES AGAINST **CHILDREN** RESEARCH CENTER

WHO Library Cataloguing-in-Publication Data

Toolkit on mapping legal, health and social services responses to child maltreatment.

1.Child Abuse – legislation and jurisprudence. 2.Child Abuse – prevention and control. 3.Social Work. 4.Child Health Services. I.World Health Organization.

ISBN 978 92 4 154907 3   (NLM classification: WA 325)

Designed by minimum graphics
Printed in Malta

Contents

Contributors

Editors
Andreas Jud, Lisa M. Jones, Christopher Mikton

Chapter I. Introduction
Authors: Andreas Jud, David Finkelhor, Lisa M. Jones, Christopher Mikton

Chapter II. Overview of previous agency surveys and national administrative data sets
Authors: Paula Krüger, Andreas Jud

Chapter 1. Agency selection
Author Section 1.1: Nico Trocmé

Author Section 1.2: Christopher Mikton

Authors Section 1.3: Andreas Jud, Andrea J. Sedlak

Chapter 2. Case selection
Author: Lisa M. Jones

Chapter 3. Definitions, variables and coding
Authors: Lisa M. Jones, Andreas Jud

Chapter 4. Statistical modelling
Author: Andreas Jud

Chapter 5. Collaboration between research and practice
Authors Section 5.1: Andreas Jud, Fadia AlBuhairan, Athanasios Ntinapogias, George Nikolaidis

Authors Section 5.2: Lenneke R. A. Alink, Saskia Euser

Authors Section 5.3: Christopher Mikton

Authors Section 5.4: Patricia Lannen

Author affiliation

Fadia AlBuhairan
National Family Safety Program and Ministry of the National Guard-Health Affairs, Riyadh, Saudi Arabia

Lenneke R. A. Alink
Child and Family Studies; Leiden University; Leiden, The Netherlands

Saskia Euser
Child and Family Studies; Leiden University; Leiden, The Netherlands

David Finkelhor
Crimes Against Children Research Center; University of New Hampshire; Durham, NH, USA

Lisa M. Jones
Crimes Against Children Research Center; University of New Hampshire; Durham, NH, USA

Andreas Jud
School of Social Work; Lucerne University of Applied Sciences and Arts; Lucerne, Switzerland

Paula Krüger
School of Social Work; Lucerne University of Applied Sciences and Arts; Lucerne, Switzerland

Patricia Lannen
UBS Optimus Foundation; Zurich, Switzerland

Christopher Mikton
Department for Management of Noncommunicable Diseases, Disability, Violence and Injury Prevention; World Health Organization; Geneva, Switzerland

George Nikolaidis
Institute of Child Health; Department of Mental Health and Social Welfare; Athens, Greece

Athanasios Ntinapogias
Institute of Child Health; Department of Mental Health and Social Welfare; Athens, Greece

Andrea J. Sedlak
Westat, Inc.; Rockville, MD, USA

Nico Trocmé
School of Social Work; McGill University; Montreal, QC, Canada

Acknowledgements

We wish to thank the authors listed above for their contributions to this publication and the many child protection experts around the globe from whose help this document has greatly benefited. In particular, we would like to thank Fadia AlBuhairan, Majid Al-Eissa, Maha Al Muneef, Lenneke R. A. Alink, Lillian Artz, Martin Chabot, Irene Cheah, Saskia Euser, Barbara Fallon, Jörg M. Fegert, Paula Krüger, Rachel Lael-Szabo, Bong Joo Lee, James Mansell, Ben Mathews, George Nikolaidis, Athanasios Ntinapogias, Hubert van Puyenbroeck and Peter Voll for their attendance at the initial expert meeting, and for their contributions to writing and editing the toolkit chapters. Special thanks go out to David Finkelhor and Nico Trocmé, who developed the initial concept for the toolkit, as well as to John Fluke and Andrea J. Sedlak, who were responsible for a significant part of the editing. We would like to thank the UBS Optimus Foundation for its generous support for the development and publication of this toolkit.

Cite as: Jud, A, Jones, L, Mikton, C. *Toolkit on mapping legal, health and social services responses to child maltreatment*. Geneva, Switzerland, World Health Organization, 2015.

I. Introduction

There is widespread agreement that in order to make progress on child maltreatment it is important for policy-makers to have information on its scope and characteristics, often referred to by the public health term "epidemiology". Researchers around the world have typically responded to this need using community surveys to count the prevalence of child maltreatment in the general population. Hundreds of such studies have been done in dozens of countries and other jurisdictions.

However, general population surveys often have limited implications for specific policies. What policy-makers often need most is information about which officials or agencies in their jurisdictions have knowledge of the problem, and what they are doing or not doing when they encounter it. Based on this information they can make concrete plans about how to change practices, train officials, and reorganize systems to better respond. They therefore need information on whether these cases are coming to the attention of school teachers or police or doctors and on what these professionals are doing. It may turn out that some officials are encountering very few cases; perhaps they need more training. It may turn out that other officials are finding cases but failing to do anything about them. Or cases that would be best dealt with by doctors are instead primarily coming to the attention of teachers but not getting referred. This knowledge helps create strategies for change. As policy-makers make changes, provide training, and raise awareness, they will then want to know if their reforms are having the desired effect.

Studies that can help policy-makers are often ones with information about what is being encountered by agencies and officials who are in positions to help and respond. In comparison to population surveys, where children and families are surveyed directly, "agency surveys" collect data from community and government organizations involved with children, such as schools, law enforcement agencies, hospitals, mental health agencies, family service agencies, nongovernmental organizations, and child protection agencies. Some well-resourced countries experienced with research collect this kind of data annually. But research studies that are done on an occasional basis or in pilot studies in jurisdictions that are in the early stages of trying to find out more about the nature of the problem can also be very informative. This toolkit is a guide to how to conduct these kinds of agency survey studies.

We believe these studies can be an incredibly important tool for helping policy-makers learn about child maltreatment in their jurisdiction and think about how to organize their response. Studies of this kind have not been conducted regularly because knowledge on how to conduct them is still developing. Because researchers are often more familiar with conducting population surveys, these have tended to be the default in research on child maltreatment. The goal of this toolkit is to provide researchers with more information on methodological strategies and considerations when conducting agency studies on child maltreatment to increase the use and success of this kind of research in countries and jurisdictions around the globe. Such research may then lead to more structured agency data collection systems to inform practice in the area of child maltreatment.

This toolkit therefore contains tips, recommended practices and resources for academics and decision-makers in child protection who are interested in conducting national or regional surveillance of agency response to child maltreatment and child maltreatment incidence through the collection of administrative data (data that is collected by professionals as part of their workload, see **BOX 1.2** in **SECTION 1.3** for more details) or through surveys of professionals.

Although findings from previous professional surveys and analyses of administrative data conducted by others are sometimes available in peer-reviewed journals, guidance on how to conduct such surveys and analyses is, to our knowledge, not available, and the experiences of investigators in collaborating with agencies and stakeholders and setting up and conducting these kinds of studies are rarely published. In this toolkit, we have gathered examples from a range of previous studies and recommendations by investigators experienced in this area. Further, we provide readers with links to additional resources on survey methodology, data analysis and dissemination.

The outline of the toolkit was drafted at a meeting of international experts in Geneva in December 2013. Participants included principle investigators of previous nationally representative agency surveys and researchers involved in developing administrative data sets on national surveillance of child maltreatment incidence. The meeting attendees and additional experts who contributed by writing and editing the toolkit chapters are listed in the acknowledgements above, and contact information is provided on the back of the cover.

While the toolkit is directed primarily at researchers in countries with fairly well-established child protection systems, it might also be useful for researchers planning surveys on the incidence of child maltreatment in countries with less-developed systems. We address this challenge, and considerations of research feasibility in these settings, in **SECTION 1.2**.

The structure of the toolkit

The toolkit aims to provide researchers with guidance for improving the quality of studies that use administrative data to better ascertain child maltreatment incidence, response and service delivery. However, these are complex studies to conduct, and the toolkit is not meant to be comprehensive. Researchers using the toolkit should be prepared to follow up on the recommended resources contained within and to consult with other professionals, such as statisticians, to further improve the research design and execution.

The chapters of the toolkit roughly follow the recommended procedural steps in planning an agency survey in the order that they might be considered by a researcher. However, decisions about one aspect of study methodology both influence and are influenced by decisions about other aspects. Because of the natural areas of overlap, and because each chapter was intended to stand alone as a source of information on each topic area, some repetitiveness in content occurs across chapters.

The introductory section is followed by an overview of previous nationally representative agency surveys and administrative data sets of national surveillance of child maltreatment incidence. The first chapter focuses on selecting agencies for your study. It starts with a framework for mapping the universe of child protection authorities in your country – an important exercise before starting to conceptualize your sampling plan. We also consider the situation of countries that lack well-developed agencies charged with responding to child maltreatment. Information is provided on how to conduct a preliminary assessment to determine if a full mapping exercise described by this is feasible. The final section in the first chapter provides an overview of strategies for sampling agencies (random sampling, stratification, etc.) and briefs the readers on calculating adjustment weights to correct for a lack of representativity of a sample. It is enriched with examples from previous agency surveys and also introduces a taxonomy of agencies.

The second chapter discusses procedures for sampling cases from within the included agencies, such as options for estimating sample frame characteristics and case flow, abstracting record data versus conducting staff surveys, and dealing with duplication issues.

The third chapter provides resources on creating forms and questionnaires for surveys by connecting readers with previously used definitions, variables and codes. It further introduces readers to the benefits and challenges of having variables and their definitions validated through research–practice partnerships.

While the major goal of nationally representative agency surveys on child maltreatment is to describe the magnitude of reported child maltreatment incidents, inferential data analyses will often have to rely on statistical modelling and advanced statistics. The fourth chapter provides a short introduction to some of the more important approaches for the field to facilitate communication with statisticians and provides researchers with information on further resources and easy-to-use readings.

Collaboration between researchers and practitioners is essential to successful participation and reliability of findings. The final chapter's first section is dedicated to strategies for successful collaboration and provides several examples from previous studies. Separate sections follow on cost issues in planning a survey and dissemination of findings. A final section is dedicated to strategies for increasing project sustainability, i.e., creating benefits to a country's child protection system for an extended period after the initial funding has ceased.

> **This toolkit will be complemented by a web appendix that connects readers with additional resources. However, we might have missed important resources, and the literature on agency response to child maltreatment is still growing. To improve the impact of the toolkit, we welcome feedback on the web appendix and suggestions for links to additional resources. Please contact the editor at andreas.jud@hslu.ch.**

II. Overview of previous agency surveys and national administrative data sets

While there is a solid body of research on measuring child maltreatment prevalence through self-report surveys (1–3), far less attention has been paid to methods for studying abuse incidence and response by surveying service agencies (4). However, a few countries, such as the Netherlands, New Zealand, and the United States of America, have collected data on how their service agencies are responding to child maltreatment, mainly using two distinct data collection strategies: professional surveys and/or administrative data extraction (5).

Possibly due to the child protection orientation[1] of their child welfare systems (6), countries like Canada and the United States started collecting data on agency response to child maltreatment much earlier than elsewhere (4). In North America, two cross-sectional professional surveys are conducted on a cyclical basis on the nature and the extent of child maltreatment: in the United States, the National Incidence Study of Child Abuse and Neglect (NIS) and, in Canada, the Canadian Incidence Study of Reported Child Abuse and Neglect (CIS) (see TABLE II.1). The NIS in the United States began in 1979. Since then four cycles have been completed, with one study conducted in each decade (NIS-1979/1980, 1986/1987, 1993/1995, 2005) (7–10). In Canada, the first CIS was published in 1998, followed by a new study every five years (CIS-1998, 2003, 2008) (11–14).

Both the NIS and the CIS rely on data obtained from nationally representative samples of child protection workers during a 3-month reference period, extrapolated to an estimate of the annual prevalence of the different types of child maltreatment in the whole country (15). Additionally, the NIS also includes survey data from frontline professionals in agencies that have frequent contact with children – for example, hospitals, day care centres, mental health agencies, and municipal police departments. The NIS refers to these professionals as "sentinels" reflecting their role in observing and helping children. These sentinels are important because they are involved in early identification of potential child abuse and make initial screening decisions about whether to alert authorities to any abuse or neglect that they suspect.

In Europe, a research team at Leiden University adapted the NIS methodology for the Netherlands with a first cycle of the nationwide prevalence study of child maltreatment (NPM) in 2005 (16). Consistent with the NIS, the study not only used data from the 15 Dutch child protective services but also recruited more than 1100 community sentinels. The agency survey component[2] of the NPM 2010 replicated the methodology of the previous cycle (17).

....

[1] For child welfare services, Gilbert (6) differs between child protection orientation (prevalent in Anglophone countries) and child and family services orientation (prevalent in continental European countries). While child protection oriented systems have a tendency to frame the problem of maltreatment in the context of harmful behaviour of malevolent parents favouring mandated reporting, investigative tracks and substantiation, systems with a child and family services orientation tend to characterize endangerment of children as stemming from psychological difficulties, marital discordance and socioeconomic stress. There, protecting families and children from maltreatment is one of a range of universal and targeted services.

[2] Both NPM-cycles were accompanied by a population survey among 12- to 17-year-old children (3, 17).

In Switzerland, the NIS methodology was adapted for a first nationwide study on child sexual victimization (18). Public child protective services, police forces, interdisciplinary hospital child protection teams and other agencies in the child protection system shared data on newly reported cases in an online data set. In contrast to the three months reference period of NIS, CIS and NPM, data from a period of six months was included. In an effort to mobilize knowledge and create research practice partnerships (see **SECTION 5.1**), a new multisite study team is attempting to improve the commitment of agencies to enhance data sharing and increase participation in a second wave of data collection, now including all types of child maltreatment.

In 2008, the Israeli government began to implement the first stage of the National Program for Children and Youth at Risk, a project designed to establish uniform definitions and improve and expand the services provided to children and youth at risk.[3] In its first phase, the programme was implemented in 72 localities in the lowest socioeconomic areas, where about 40% of the children in Israel live. The implementation of the programme was accompanied by an agency survey (19) including universal services (family health clinics, preschools, elementary and high schools) and community treatment agencies (social services departments, youth probation services, truancy services and youth advancement sections). Data were gathered by professionals using an online form. Since 2008, the project has expanded and currently covers about two thirds of Israel's child population.

Unlike the previously mentioned surveys that relied on professionals completing paper or online survey or data collection forms, the Balkan Epidemiological Study on Child Abuse and Neglect (BECAN) (20)[4] used a slightly different strategy to collect data. In this study, local research teams involved in nine case-based surveillance studies in south-eastern European nations (Albania, Bosnia and Herzegovina, Bulgaria, Croatia, Greece, Romania, Serbia, the former Yugoslav Republic of Macedonia and Turkey) abstracted data directly from agency case files. The age range was restricted to children aged 11, 13 and 16 years. **SECTION 5.1** describes in more detail the procedures this study used for collecting data and obtaining agency commitment.

In addition to all the above surveys collecting data on individual child maltreatment cases, there are other studies which analyse aggregate data (versus case-level data) (21). Currently, two new nationally representative agency surveys are under way – in the Dominican Republic and South Africa.[5] The South African study combines a population survey of adolescents with a survey on child maltreatment reported to agencies and will explore gaps in reporting and the services offered to child victims.[6]

Examples of child maltreatment research using nationally representative administrative data sets are particularly rare. In the United States, a national database on children and families who come to the attention of state public child welfare agencies was created. Child protection agencies across the United States systematically enter child maltreatment case data into online databases. States then regularly submit these data to the National Child Abuse and Neglect Data System (NCANDS). Reports summarizing these data have been published annually since the system began in 1990 (22–24). Participation of individual states in the NCANDS system is voluntary, but funding incentives for system development has motivated

---

3   As only limited information is available in English, this section is partly derived from personal communication with Rachel Szabo-Lael.

4   The BECAN webpage (www.becan.eu/node/33) provides a global report and nine national reports.

5   Please contact Henry Parada, Ryerson University, Toronto, ON, Canada, at hparada@ryerson.ca for information on the Dominican Republic study.

6   Information on the South African study was provided by Lillian Artz (personal communication, October 21, 2014). Results are expected in late 2015 and will be available at http://www.optimusstudy.org/index.php?id=262.

TABLE II.1

Overview of nationally representative agency surveys on agency response to child maltreatment[a]

TITLE	COUNTRY	REFERENCE PERIOD	TYPE(S) AND NUMBER OF AGENCIES INCLUDED (MOST RECENT CYCLE)	TYPE OF CHILD MALTREATMENT
Canadian Incidence Study of Reported Child Abuse and Neglect (CIS)	Canada	1998, 2003, 2008 [3-month period]	112 child protective services	any
National Incidence Study of Child Abuse and Neglect (NIS)	United States	1979/1980, 1986/1987, 1993/1995, 2005/2006 [3-month period]	126 child protective services and 1094 sentinel agencies (county sheriff departments, county departments of juvenile probation, public health, and public housing, and samples of municipal police departments, hospitals, shelters, day care centres, schools, other social services and mental health agencies)	any
National Program for Children and Youth at Risk	Israel	2008–2014	2014 data collection in 160 localities, covering about two thirds of Israel's child population; included are universal services (family health clinics, preschools, elementary and high schools) and community treatment agencies (social services departments, youth probation services, truancy services and youth advancement sections)	any [plus further adverse childhood experiences]
The Netherlands Prevalence Study on Maltreatment of Children and Youths (NPM)	Netherlands	2005, 2010 [3-month period]	15 child protective services and 416 sentinel agencies (schools, day care centres, well-baby clinics, general practitioners, emergency department workers, child protection professionals in hospitals, shelters for battered women, police forces, child protection boards)	any
Optimus Study Agency Survey	Switzerland	2010 [6-month period]	345 child protective services and sentinel agencies (police departments, (juvenile) prosecution agencies, hospitals, mental health agencies, school psychological services, victim aid agencies, private agencies specialized in supporting victims of child sexual abuse)	child sexual victimization

[a] The surveys are not restricted to a specific age group.

participation. For the most recent report, all 50 states, the District of Columbia, and Puerto Rico reported data on their child protective services' response to child maltreatment (24).

There are other national administrative data sets:

▶ In New Zealand, the Child, Youth and Family Service (CYF) formally responds to child maltreatment for the whole country (25). Since 1992 all data on child protection have been collected in the National Child Protection Case Management System (26). The system is updated on a daily basis.

▶ A similar data set is available in the Republic of Korea. The national child protection authority, founded in 2001, administers a central database of all reports of maltreatment to the 51 current local child protection agencies[7] (4, 27).

▶ Since 2006, Germany collects data nationally on the caseload of all public child welfare agencies, including information on alleged child maltreatment. However, only a small portion of the caseload includes information on child maltreatment, as parents have a legal right to child and youth welfare services (such as counselling, family preservation or placement services) even when child maltreatment is not an issue (4). Unfortunately, an international audience has only limited access to the findings, as most of the analyses have been conducted for internal purposes and the findings published only in German.[8]

▶ In Saudi Arabia, the National Child Abuse and Neglect Registry (NCANR) is located in the health sector (28). All child protection centres at major hospitals – established as part of the National Family Safety Program in 2007 – report to the registry. Obtaining collaboration for national surveillance of child maltreatment incidence in Saudi Arabia is detailed in **SECTION 5.1**.

▶ Surveillance data on 'children in need'[9] are collected and published independently by each of the four countries in the United Kingdom of Great Britain and Northern Ireland (29). Disaggregate data have been reported since 2008–2009 (for England, see (29)) and 2012–2013 (for Scotland, see (30)). For children who are the subject of a child protection plan or are placed on the child protection register, information on types of child maltreatment is available. However, also due to variations in definitions the relative number or percentage of children classified as suffering, or likely to suffer each maltreatment type varies between the four countries (31).

▶ Recently, Australia advanced from provincial data sets on child maltreatment incidence to a national minimum data set of child protection. The 5-year period of development and implementation resulted in the first national reporting in 2012–2013 (32).[10] Analyses are not restricted to child protection services: statistical linkage keys shared with national data collections for the youth justice system and homelessness services enable information on the case outcomes of children and/or their use of health and other community services to be provided.

....

[7] The current number of local child protection agencies has been provided by Bong Joo Lee (personal communication, October 12, 2014)

[8] The data sets are accessible for German researchers on http://www.forschungsdatenzentrum.de/bestand/ jugendhilfe/index.asp; analyses are available in German at http://www.akjstat.uni-dortmund.de/.

[9] A child in need is defined under the Children Act 1989 as a child who is unlikely to reach or maintain a satisfactory level of health or development, or their health or development will be significantly impaired, without the provision of services, or the child is disabled (29).

[10] However, as two of the eight jurisdictions still chose to report aggregate data due to competing priorities, the picture is not complete.

▶ In Belgium, disaggregated administrative data collection is not unified nationally. However, in relation to the Flemish community (Flanders), the annual Child and Family Agency's compendium "The Child in Flanders" summarizes data reports of child maltreatment allegations made to the Confidential Child Abuse Centres since 1998 (33).[11]

Many other continental European countries have data on the services provided by public child welfare agencies (as would be expected within a child and family services orientation). However, these data sets either completely lack information on child maltreatment or lack reliable information, as agencies are not mandated to collect this information. Examples of data sets of child protection orders can be found in France[12] or Switzerland (34). For the French system, plans are underway to develop a comprehensive administrative data collection programme, which is now being piloted in some administrative units (named départements in France).

Although this review is not exhaustive, it supports the argument that the number of studies using professional surveys and administrative data to study child maltreatment incidence and response is still limited. This is the case not only for low- or middle-income countries but also for high-income countries. Furthermore, regional differences in data collection strategies and maltreatment definitions make comparison of the reported incidence rates difficult. In addition to the impact of different systems orientations (see above), Jud et al. (4) identified other possible obstacles to data collection on child maltreatment incidence: First, in developing nations, scarce resources might be one of the most important barriers; another might be a lack of recognition of the problem, a factor that might also apply to high-income countries, as for example, the relatively short history of child protection in the Republic of Korea indicates. Finally, in countries without a centrally organized child welfare system, the complexity of these systems seems to be a significant hurdle with respect to collecting data on child maltreatment. This holds especially true for federally organized countries like Switzerland or Germany. Yet, the NIS demonstrates that regional differences in child protection systems can be handled through creative methodological means (35), and the toolkit presented here offers general guidelines for tackling such methodological issues.

Further resources

Australian Institute of Health and Welfare
Further details on the Child Protection National Minimum Data Set and reports on child protection Australia can be found at http://www.aihw.gov.au/child-protection-publications/

Canadian Child Welfare Research Portal
Reports and secondary analyses of the CIS cycles are available at http://cwrp.ca – among many other resources on child welfare research in Canada and beyond.

Children's Bureau at the United States' Department of Health and Human Services
Annual reports on the NCANDS data set are provided on the webpage of the Children's Bureau at http://www.acf.hhs.gov/programs/cb/research-data-technology/statistics-research/child-maltreatment

....

[11] Each annual compendium with detailed data-based information on all child-related issues in Flanders is available through http://www.kindengezin.be/algemeen/english-pages.jsp. Reports to child protective services in the French-speaking region are available in French through http://www.one.be/index.php?id=rapports-one.
[12] The national observatory on endangered children in France (ONED) provides some publications in English, see http://www.oned.gouv.fr/ressources/?profil=263.

Kind en Gezin, Flanders

English versions of the annual reports on reported child maltreatment in Flanders are available at http://www.kindengezin.be/algemeen/english-pages.jsp

Leiden Attachment Research Program

English summaries and the full Dutch reports on the NPM cycles are available on the webpage of the research programme at http://www.leidenattachmentresearchprogram.eu

National Data Archive on Child Abuse and Neglect Data (NDACAN)

In the United States, the NDACAN not only houses previous cycles of the annual nationwide administrative data collection NCANDS but also acquires microdata from leading United States researchers and makes these datasets available to the research community for secondary analysis. NDACAN supports information-sharing through its Child Maltreatment Research List Serve and provides data analysis opportunities to researchers through conference workshops and its annual Summer Research Institute. See http://www.ndacan.cornell.edu/

National Incidence Study of Child Abuse and Neglect (NIS)

As a new feature, the webpage of the NIS provides access to the data set of the most recent cycle for live analyses at https://www.nis4.org

Surveillance statistics on child maltreatment incidence in the United Kingdom

The four countries of the United Kingdom collect and publish data independently. The following links lead to the most recent reports for each country.

England: https://www.gov.uk/government/statistics/characteristics-of-children-in-need-in-england-2012-to-2013

Scotland: http://www.scotland.gov.uk/Topics/Statistics/Browse/Children/PubChildrenSocialWork

Wales: http://wales.gov.uk/statistics-and-research/wales-children-need-census/?lang=en

Northern Ireland: http://www.dhsspsni.gov.uk/index/stats_research/stats-cib-3/statistics_and_research-cib-pub/children_statistics/stats-cib-children_order.htm

1. Agency selection

1.1 Mapping child protection agencies

In jurisdictions where detailed case-level child protection investigation data are not readily available in a centralized database, in particular in instances where multiple child protection agencies manage their own data using different information systems, multistage sampling can be used to select a representative sample of agencies and then select cases within agencies. Agency selection starts with developing a sampling frame, i.e. a list of all the organizations that respond to concerns related to suspected child abuse or neglect. These may include specifically mandated organizations such as the police and child protection agencies as well as other types of organizations such as hospitals or mental health agencies. The sampling frame may further include individuals such as community physicians or school counsellors. Constructing the list of agencies can prove to be a challenge. It is usually fairly simple to obtain a list of authorities in countries with state-run specialized agencies supported by mandatory reporting laws and investigation regulations (10, 15), but it can prove to be far more difficult in countries where there is no centralized government structure that mandates reporting and investigation or assessment responsibilities (4). Even in countries with relatively centralized protection investigation systems, some subpopulations, for instance religious minorities or indigenous populations, may operate their own response systems outside of the mainstream structure of child protection authorities (36). The purpose of this chapter is to propose a mapping framework that recognizes the range and diversity of formal to informal organizations that carry out child abuse and neglect investigations.

1.1.1 Defining the child protection organization sampling unit

One of the challenges inherent in developing a list of child protection agencies is that the very concept of child protection varies considerably from one country to another and, in some countries, from one state or province to another. In comparing child protection systems across several high-income countries, Gilbert and colleagues (37, 38) identified two broad approaches to child protection: a child safety approach (the primary model in North America and Australia) and a child and family welfare approach (the model in, for example, England, Germany, New Zealand and Sweden). Differences between the two approaches include: (1) the extent to which service providing organizations are limited to dealing with child protection or whether service providers cover a broader range of child and family problems, (2) whether there are mandatory reporting laws in place, (3) the extent to which assessments focus more narrowly on risk of maltreatment or more broadly on child and family needs, and (4) the scope of services provided, with child safety oriented systems tending to be focused on investigation and short-term services and child and family welfare systems tending to offer a broader array of services, often over a longer term basis. To address some of the challenges inherent in confronting child maltreatment, both approaches have been borrowing from each other, making the distinction between the child safety and child and family welfare approaches more difficult to establish (38).

Mapping child protection agencies is generally a simpler task in systems with a child safety orientation. In these more closely regulated child protection systems, all reports of suspected child abuse or neglect are sent to mandated child protection organizations that process the reports in a standardized way (10, 39). Even in instances where some components of the investigation may be carried out by specialized hospital-based units or in children's advocacy centres, case management typically rests with the mandated child protection organization. In these instances it is fairly straight forward to obtain a list of all organizations that conduct child protection investigations, to the extent that cases fit within the mandate of these organizations. However, careful attention should be paid to understanding the scope of these organizations as set by legislated mandates. In Canada, for example, mandates vary considerably by province: some provinces limit investigations to children under the age of 16 years, but others extend the scope of investigations to youth up to 18 years of age; some provinces specifically include exposure to intimate partner violence, and others do not (39) (see also http://www.cwrp.ca). It should also be noted that in many systems, extra-familial cases of abuse where there are no concerns about parental supervision might only be investigated by the police.

In jurisdictions that have a less regulated and more flexible approach – an approach that may very well be better tailored to a range of child and family needs – mapping out the pathways from detection to reporting to investigation may prove to be more difficult (4). The very concept of a 'child maltreatment investigation' could be quite different in these jurisdictions. In more severe cases of maltreatment, for instance cases involving contact child sexual abuse or physical abuse with serious injuries, it may be relatively simple to identify which authorities are mandated to conduct an investigation – the police, for instance. However, the label of maltreatment may not be used as readily in jurisdictions using a broader child and family welfare approach, because this label is not necessarily an entry point to accessing services. In cases involving a mix of concerns about parenting, family dysfunction, extreme poverty and child difficulties, there is likely to be significant variation in the extent to which child maltreatment labels, such as neglect or emotional maltreatment, are used. In these instances, the very concept of a 'report' or an 'investigation' may be difficult to ascertain, when a 'referral' or a 'request for services' and an 'assessment' may in fact better describe the front end of these services. As a result of this broader approach, the task of mapping child protection organizations is complicated by the fact that many different child and family service organizations can be involved in assessing maltreatment, ranging from the police, services run by local government social services, and hospital-based child abuse and neglect teams, to charitable organizations and private clinics.

Although child protection services in Canada are generally considered to be fairly closely regulated and child safety oriented, our experience in conducting the Canadian Incidence Studies of Reported Child Abuse and Neglect (36, 39) shows that mapping out the list of organizations responsible for investigating child maltreatment poses unexpected challenges. A growing number of jurisdictions have developed differential response models designed to provide a more flexible service response, which may involve streaming less urgent cases of reported maltreatment to specialized teams or community agencies (40). Even when differential response models are not formally deployed, we have found that some Aboriginal agencies use more of a child and family welfare approach, where it can be difficult to distinguish between a report, a referral and an informal request for assistance (36). Likewise, determining which organizations are mandated to investigate maltreatment has been a challenge, as mainstream government-mandated child protection organizations delegate a growing range of child protection responsibilities to Aboriginal agencies.

The structure and delivery of child protection services varies considerably from one jurisdiction to another and, upon closer inspection, may vary in unexpected ways within jurisdictions. The task of constructing a sampling frame of all child protection organizations in a particular jurisdiction requires a thorough understanding of the structures and mandates governing a range of organizations that conduct child maltreatment investigations or assessments. Even in child safety oriented systems with mandatory reporting laws and centrally organized child protection services, careful attention needs to be given to 'exceptions to the rule', including what types of maltreatment fall under which mandates, which subgroups might have access to alternate service delivery systems, and which age-groups are covered by which systems.

1.1.2 Child protection mapping framework

To facilitate the task of mapping out child protection organizations, we propose that researchers consider three key dimensions: (1) level of authority, (2) function, and (3) reporting process. **FIG. 1.1** shows these three mapping dimensions. The level of authority varies from a centralized legislated and regulated child protection system, to decentralized but legally mandated systems, to organizations that receive reports as part of their professional mandates, to traditional authorities such as village elders or tribal leaders. The function of the authorities receiving reports ranges from helping, to protecting, to prosecuting. Finally, the role of these levels of authorities and their function will vary depending on the point in the reporting process where sampling may occur: from receipt of a report, to screening, to investigating, to making a determination, to intervening.

Source of authority

When serious concerns arise about parental care, societies have developed a range of more or less formal and structured mechanisms to address a child's need for protection. The level of structure and formality defining child protection authority can be classified on a continuum

Fig. 1.1 Dimensions of organization of child protection systems

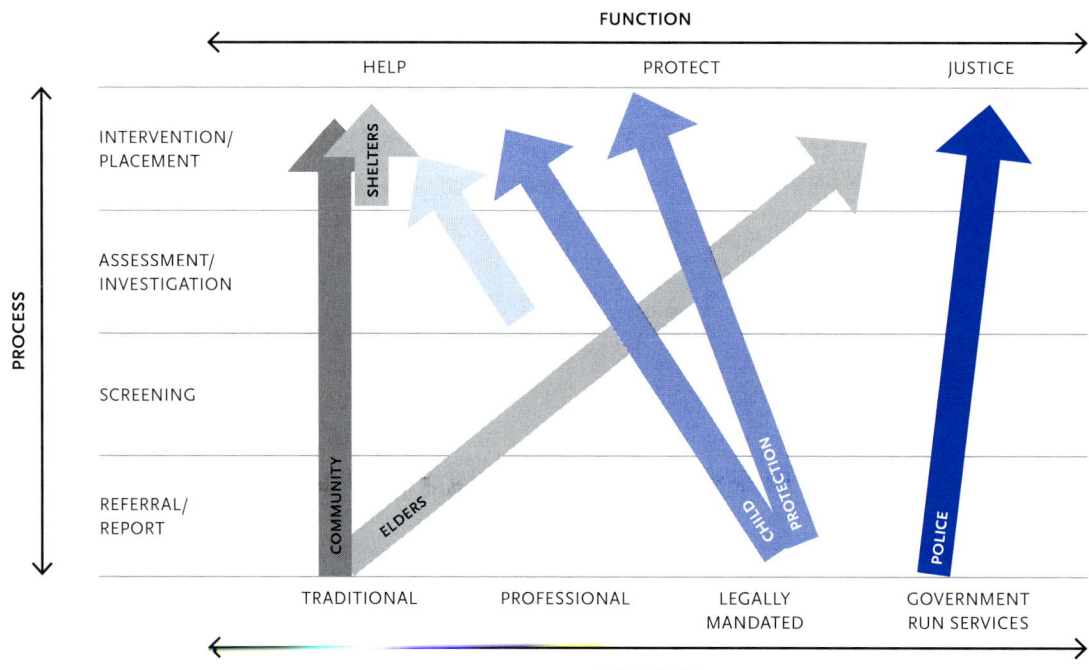

ranging from traditional community-based structures, to professionally mandated authorities, to legally mandated ones, to government-run protection services.

▶ **Traditional authorities**

In the absence of more formal government-mandated authorities, the head of a family clan, a council of elders or local political or religious leaders may serve as the local authorities for resolving serious family conflicts or intervening when the care of a child does not meet community standards. Even if such traditional authorities are not formally sanctioned or recognized by government, it would be a mistake to overlook them if they are de facto serving a child protection function.

▶ **Professional mandates**

Health, education and social welfare professionals operate with their own code of ethics or work in organizations that may have rules with respect to child protection. Even if their potential child protection role is not regulated through a legislated government mandate, their professional or organizational codes of ethics may very well require them to take measures in response to suspected child maltreatment. As with traditional authorities, professionals may also play an important protective function in jurisdictions where child protection legislation is minimal or there is limited implementation infrastructure.

▶ **Legally mandated nongovernmental organizations**

In many jurisdictions the legislated mandate to respond to child protection concerns is delegated to community-based organizations. In Ontario, Canada, for example, the receipt of reports, mandate to investigate and powers to remove a child are delegated by the government to local not-for-profit "Children's Aid Societies". These agencies are typically organized on a geographical basis but several cover populations defined through religious (Catholic or Jewish) or Aboriginal status. In Switzerland, the authority to investigate and the mandate to provide services is even further decentralized, with a mix of public and private agencies structured in different ways in each of the 26 cantons.

▶ **Government-run protection services**

In the case of government-run services, protection authorities are in principle easily identified through the government service delivery structure. This is the most straightforward when child protection functions rest with a dedicated department or service, although it is less so when government departments or services cover a range of functions, such as a generic social services department where staff carry mixed caseloads.

Function

Related to a certain extent to the source of authority, function will also affect what types of organizations are included in mapping out child protection activities. Three primary functions drive the structure of child protections systems: helping, protecting and dispensing justice. Most organizations serve more than one of these functions, but in mapping out the structure of protection systems it is important to clarify which types of functions a study is being designed to document.

▶ **Helping**

We refer here to the broader term of helping rather than treatment in order to include non-professional help and support that may be provided through extended family and community. Although one might expect that all child protection services are designed to provide treatment services, many in fact are focused on investigation and case management activities, with treatment functions being contracted out to specialized agencies. Organizations that play a helping function, such as children's mental health centres, therapeutic treatment programmes, or some children's advocacy centres, include specific individual family or group treatment services designed to mitigate the effects of maltreatment and minimize the risk of re-victimization. Some protection systems include investigation and treatment services within the same organization, and others access services from specialized treatment organizations.

In child safety oriented systems, treatment services are often tertiary level services accessed through post-investigation referrals, and a finding of maltreatment may be a condition of receiving services. In contrast, in child and family welfare oriented systems, a request for treatment may be the first point of contact, and, if there are no mandatory reporting laws and no concerns that may require judicial or police intervention, the provision of treatment services may be the only protection activity involved. In Germany, for example, "parents have a legal right to child and youth welfare services (e.g. counselling, family preservation or placement services) even when child maltreatment is not an issue" (4). If parents are not willing or unable to address the child's needs, child welfare services can opt for intensified protective activities by referring the case to family court.

▶ Protecting

The protection function is central to the organization of services in child safety oriented systems. The focus of these services is first and foremost on preventing recurrence of maltreatment through protective activities. In situations where a child can be kept at home safely, protection takes the form of supervising the home situation to ensure that parents have made the changes required to ensure the child's safety. The alternative is removal of the child from the home, either on a temporary basis until the home is deemed safe again or on a permanent basis. Treatment services may also be provided, but the primary focus is to monitor the child's safety.

▶ Dispensing Justice

Whereas helping and protecting are generally thought of as being the central components of a child protection system, the police and the courts, as well as traditional leaders, serve a justice function through criminal proceedings or some type of restitution process. Even in centralized child safety-focused systems, some forms of child victimization, such as extra-familial sexual abuse or physical assault by non-family members, may be dealt with solely through police investigations. In many of these situations, if there are no concerns about the family's ability to support and protect the child, child protection authorities will not be notified. Thus, a complete list of organizations responsible for conducting child maltreatment investigations may need to include the police.

Process

In mapping out child protection organizations one also has to consider at what stage of the process services need to be tracked. Counts of child protection case activities range from numbers of reports, to numbers of investigations, to numbers of substantiated reports, to numbers of children placed in out-of-home care. Because some organizations are only involved in parts of this process, one must clearly delineate which types of activities need to be mapped. The response to child protection concerns can be classified in terms of three key processes: receiving a report/referral, investigating/assessing, and intervening.

▶ **Report/refer**

In more structured child safety oriented systems with mandatory reporting laws, specific organizations are mandated to receive reports. In jurisdictions with a child and family welfare orientation, the concept of a 'report' may be limited to the most severe forms of maltreatment, whereas situations involving a range of child and family problems may instead be referred for support or counselling services without going through a report.

▶ **Investigate/assess**

In a similar fashion, the assessment process will have more of an investigative form in child safety oriented systems, whereas it may be more of a needs assessment in a child and family welfare oriented system. Different types of investigation may involve different types of organizations, with criminal investigations conducted by the police, some forensic investigations by specialized medical units, and safety and protection investigations conducted by protection authorities. As a result, mapping out which organizations are involved in investigating or assessing child protection concerns requires a good understanding of these different potential processes. In child and family welfare oriented systems the distinction between a protection investigation and a child and family assessment may be more difficult to establish.

▶ **Intervention/placement**

As noted earlier, the organizations that receive reports and conduct investigations are not necessarily the same as the organizations that provide services. In some instances services might be contracted out to other community organizations or community professionals; in others the same organization is responsible for all three levels. Finally, some organizations, like shelters for street youth, may provide support and counselling directly to victimized youth without being part of the reporting and investigation sequence.

1.1.3 Conclusions

Constructing a sampling frame of child protection organizations is a key step in conducting any child protection agency survey. The framework that we propose in this chapter is designed around a broad understanding of the full range of formal to informal systems that are designed to respond to situations where serious concerns about parental care, including abuse and neglect, may require some type of intervention. In many instances this mapping process should be viewed as a study in and of itself requiring dedicated resources and timeframe to ensure that the full spectrum of child protection agencies and related organizations are accurately represented.

1.2 Preliminary assessment to determine if the full mapping exercise is warranted

Before embarking on a fully-fledged study to map the legal, health and social services responses to child maltreatment, it will sometimes be advisable to conduct a preliminary assessment to determine if such a mapping exercise is warranted. This will, in particular, be the case in low- and middle-income countries that lack well-developed formal agencies charged with responding to child maltreatment or in which such agencies are only nascent. This preliminary assessment is probably superfluous in many high-income countries with long-established and well-developed child protection services. Conversely, in some – particularly low-income – countries where child protection services either do not exist or are still in an embryonic state with very limited reach, such a mapping exercise may turn out to be premature.

Tempting though it might be, trying to develop a single checklist of hard-and-fast criteria for when it is warranted to undertake such a mapping exercise is not feasible: first, because there are too many different research questions such a mapping exercise might try to answer, and second, because it would be extremely difficult to support it empirically. So instead, we will suggest different categories of information that should be considered in the course of a rapid preliminary assessment to help determine whether or not it is worthwhile undertaking the full mapping exercise. The results of the preliminary assessment can contribute to planning the full mapping exercise, should the decision be made to proceed with it.

Step 1 – Formulating research questions: The first step is to clearly formulate the research question or questions that the mapping exercise is intended to answer. There are at least three types of questions such a mapping exercise can help answer, each with – as indicated below – many possible subsidiary questions:

1. What is the current state of development of the legal, health and social services agencies responding to child maltreatment in the country? The state of development of such agencies includes dimensions such as the level of funding for such agencies; the number and level of training of staff of such agencies; and their coverage (e.g. geographic, types of cases, and types of populations served), accessibility, and quality. This question can have several related aims, including:

    i.   to assess the success and extent of the implementation of a national policy, strategy, or plan to develop child protection services in a country;

    ii. to establish a baseline measure against which the future development of child protection services can be tracked;

    iii. to track future progress against an already existing baseline measure.

2. What is the nature of agencies responding to child maltreatment and the nature of their response?

    i.   Which kinds of agencies are responding to child maltreatment? This might include questions such as:

         • Which sector are they part of? Health, justice, social welfare, education, other?

         • What kinds of organizations are they? Governmental, nongovernmental, community-based, faith-based, private foundations, international organizations, informal or customary authorities?

    ii. Who is responding to child maltreatment within these agencies? Professionals, para-professionals, non professionals? If professionals, which professional groups? Social workers, health professionals, lawyers, paralegals, others?

    iii. What kinds of responses are they providing? Detection and investigation, health or psychosocial assessment, forensic assessment? Support, treatment and rehabilitation for victim and family, including physical and mental health services (e.g. ongoing medical care, trauma therapy, individual or family counselling); social services (e.g. respite care; assistance with everyday home tasks, foster placement; supervision by child protection services); educational services (e.g. special schooling or training); legal services (e.g. prosecution of perpetrators; child protection); and financial assistance (e.g. victim compensation funds)?

    iv. What is the coverage (e.g. geographic and types of populations served) of such agencies and the services that they provide?

    v. What is the quality of their response? To what extent are the services that they offer informed by evidence?

    vi. What is the nature of their caseload (type of child maltreatment, number of cases, demographic characteristics of cases, etc.)?

3. What is the incidence of reports of child maltreatment in the country, based on the data collected by the agencies responding to child maltreatment? It is important to note that the number of cases being seen by agencies does not define the full scope of the problem in the country, yet it is a critical planning and policy tool. For instance, it estimated that in Canada, the United Kingdom and the United States only some 5%–10% of maltreatment cases come to the attention of the authorities (*38*). In Hong Kong, China, a recent study suggests this percentage is 0.3% (*41*), and in low- and middle-income countries the fraction may be smaller still – when, that is, child protection services exist. Agency surveys should be designed to measure the response to child maltreatment in a country for planning and policy purpose, whereas population-based surveys are designed to measure actual rates of victimization, and are often less useful for planning and policy purposes.

4. Deciding on a final research question is likely to be an iterative process, with initial questions revised in the light of the findings of the preliminary assessment and the preliminary assessment being adjusted as research questions evolve.

Step 2 – Conducting a rapid assessment: If there are doubts about how well-established and developed the legal, health and social services tasked with responding are within the country, conducting a rapid assessment is recommended to determine if it is worth conducting research to answer your questions. This exercise should take between a few days and two weeks and should draw on two main sources of information:

1. existing documents, such as laws, policies, reports, published research studies, and media reports;

2. interviews with 'key informants', or individuals who have or are likely to have in-depth knowledge of child protection and child maltreatment prevention in the country. These may include policy-makers; programme planners, commissioners, and implementers; high-level practitioners; high-level civil servants and their senior technical advisers; leaders, champions, advocates, and politicians with a strong interest in the subject; and academics and researchers. They may come from many different sectors and types of organizations involved in child maltreatment prevention and child protection, including the health, social welfare/social development, education and criminal justice sectors and governmental ministries and departments, nongovernmental and community-based organizations, international organizations, and universities and other research institutions (*42*). In countries made up of different linguistic, ethnic, cultural or religious groups, it will be critical to make sure all major groups are well represented among key informants.

This rapid assessment will require a small team of two to three people – ideally composed of core members of the team who intend to carry out the full mapping exercise – having expertise in child protection and maltreatment prevention. The rapid assessment should aim to collect and synthesize information of the types listed below. These categories of information have been drawn from various instruments that have been developed to assess the readiness or capacity of countries to address various health and social problems, including child maltreatment (*43*). The information collected will have to be tailored to the specific research questions selected.

1. Scientific data on child maltreatment, such as:

   - data on magnitude and distribution of child maltreatment (e.g. prevalence and incidence studies) and any data on agency responses to child maltreatment (which even in many high-income countries are often lacking (4));

   - country-specific short- and long-term consequences of child maltreatment;

   - country-specific risk and protective factors for child maltreatment.

2. Existing surveillance and any other information systems for child maltreatment, including official definitions of child maltreatment in use and types of reporting systems (mandatory, nonmandatory, procedures for compiling and centralizing data collected, etc.).

3. Legislation, mandates, policies, and plans relevant to child protection and child maltreatment prevention, such as:

   - example of such legislation are Children's Acts (e.g. Kenya, South Africa, United Kingdom), Child Abuse Prevention and Treatment Act (United States);

   - agencies and authorities officially mandated with child protection or child maltreatment prevention; using the framework developed in **SECTION 1.1**, they can range from traditional authorities, to professional mandates and legally mandated nongovernmental organizations, through to government-run protection services. They might also include nonmandated nongovernmental, community-based organizations, or even international organizations.

   - national or subnational policies, strategies, or action plans relevant to child protection and child maltreatment – both their existence and the degree of their implementation.

4. Strength of will to address the problem of child maltreatment through prevention and response measures. The strength of will to address the problem in the country can be gauged by examining:

   - leadership on the issue, i.e. how concerned are the political, religious, business, traditional, civil society and other leaders in the country with child maltreatment, and if there is an agency, specialist office or unit in government or outside government, or a national committee that takes the lead in child protection and child maltreatment prevention (see **BOX 1.1**).

   - political will, i.e. are there political leaders who express strong commitment to the issue and are taking effective measures to address the problem, and is there an agency, specialist office or unit in government or outside government that takes the lead in this area?

   - public will, i.e. how serious a problem does the general public perceive child maltreatment to be?

   - advocacy and communication, i.e. how intensive have advocacy and communication efforts been for child protection and child maltreatment prevention?

5. Preliminary mapping of the response to child maltreatment. At this stage, this should only consist of a rapid scan or scoping exercise, but it will prepare the ground for the full mapping of agencies to be carried out if the decision is taken, on the basis of the rapid assessment, to carry out the full study. Information should be collected on the sectors, organizations (private and public, governmental and nongovernmental, etc.), and agencies responding to child maltreatment.

BOX 1.1

Strength of will to address the problem: the child protection movement in the Philippines

The success of the child protection movement in the Philippines, which has been able to secure strong political, religious and civil society support, has been due in large part to the creation of the Committee for the Special Protection of Children (CSPC), an interagency committee established by the anti-child abuse law in the Philippines. All agencies that deal with children are represented on this committee, which is co-chaired by the Departments of Justice and of Social Welfare and Development. The members of the CSPC are the Departments of Education, Health, Labour and Employment, Interior and Local Government, Tourism, and Foreign Affairs; the Commission on Human Rights and Immigration; the Philippine National Police and the National Bureau of Investigation; the Prosecutor General and three representatives of nongovernmental or private organizations working and/or advocating for the protection of children. The nongovernmental organizations represented on the committee are the Child Protection Network Foundation; End Child Prostitution, Child Pornography and Trafficking of Children for Sexual Purposes (ECPAT); and Philink (an interfaith organization). The CSPC secretariat is based in the Council for the Welfare of Children, which is responsible for harmonizing children's programmes and policies in the country. CSPC was tasked by law to come up with the comprehensive programme for child protection. The strength of CSPC derives from the support that it receives from its member agencies and from the continuity of its membership. The Philippine government's openness to the participation of nongovernmental organizations in policy-making, innovation and leadership has played a critical role in the success of the child protection movement in the country.

a. Sources for information on agencies responding to child maltreatment may come from:

- available lists or directories of agencies in the health, social welfare, educational and legal sectors, and may include governmental ministries and departments; nongovernmental, community- and faith-based organizations; international organizations; private foundations – either in print or from the Internet;

- key informants, as described above;

- research studies and reports.

b. Information should include:

- coverage of child maltreatment response agencies, in terms of geography, high-risk and special populations (children with disabilities, indigenous populations, migrant and ethnic minority populations), equality of access, and cultural sensitivity;

- resources within these sectors, organizations, and agencies dedicated to the issue, such as on overall budgets and personnel.

6. Human and technical resources required for child protection and child maltreatment prevention. Information should focus on, for instance, the number of professionals specializing in child protection and child maltreatment prevention and the number of institutions that provide training and education in this area.

7. Length of time there has been a structured, well-funded, and politically adequate support for the response to child maltreatment. In many cases, countries enact or adopt child welfare or protection laws and policies that remain largely unimplemented due to lack of capacity or political and financial support (27).

It is possible to derive approximate criteria from these different categories of information to determine when it is warranted to proceed with a mapping to answer specific research questions. For instance, if the aim is to map the nature of what is assumed to be well-developed legal, health and social services agencies responding to child maltreatment and the nature of their response, one could decide that it is only worth doing this if the preliminary assessment shows that there are officially mandated government child protection agencies, if the country has been responding to child maltreatment in a structured way for at least 10 years, that agencies cover at least 50% of the population of children, and that agencies are adequately funded. However, formulating such criteria will be largely dependent on the research question of interest.

1.3 Agency sampling

Internationally and sometimes even at the national level, there is a large variety of agencies responding to child maltreatment and an abundance of titles and terms. The process of mapping the agencies in a nation's child protection system (44) is essential to better understand the threshold of disclosing an event of victimization to a formal institution, the degree of an agency's specialization, the connections and processes between agencies, etc. In addition to the typology of agencies based on their source of authority (see SECTION 1.1), we refer in this report – for improved international comparability – to a typology with seven categories. This second taxonomy is primarily based on the professional domains of service provision that the agency is related to and should encompass all major agency stakeholders responding to child maltreatment. The categories are relatively broad, however, and further subdivisions might be needed to better portray a national child protection system. We strongly recommend that the process of mapping the agency be preferably combined with gathering information on the data already collected at the agency:

▶ **public child protection**

Refers to any type of public agency responsible for protecting children in need or at risk. Based on national or provincial legislation, the agencies are organized at the respective level. In some countries (e.g., most continental European nations), the tasks of public child protection are divided between an authority enacting child protection orders and agencies providing mandated or voluntary services. A widely used term in English publications is 'child protective services' (CPS).

▶ **law enforcement**

Refers to the state or nation's penal branch, police forces, agencies of prosecution, penal courts, correctional facilities, probation departments. It may include a separate sector of juvenile justice for offenders below the age of majority.

▶ **medical agencies and practitioners**

Refers to any medical organization for children and youth, e.g. hospitals, medical centres, well-baby clinics, and also to general practitioners.

▶ **mental health services**

Refers to any type of mental health service–whether focused on psychiatric counselling and therapy or clinical psychology–agency or private practice.

▶ **schools and school services**

Refers to any school or kindergarten, private or public, and to school services, e.g. school social workers, school psychological services.

▶ **day or residential care facility, shelters**

Refers to any agency providing care for children on a daily basis or longer period. Shelters (e.g., shelters for battered women) are also included in this category.

▶ **psychosocial counselling and social services**

Refers to any type of voluntary psychosocial counselling or social service (exempted are agencies that already qualify for categories listed above). It may include community services, private organizations specialized in combatting child maltreatment, multidisciplinary counselling services for professionals confronted with child maltreatment, and others.

Due to the focal role of public child protection, some studies dichotomize agencies into CPS and sentinel agencies (*10, 17*). However, this partially excludes the penal branch responsible for prosecution and eventual conviction of a perpetrator of child maltreatment. The next step of sampling the agencies will be shaped by the mapping of the context and the research question. The examples used to illustrate the process of agency sampling are all drawn from professional surveys. The use of administrative records to analyse the issue of incidence of child maltreatment is addressed in a separate box (**BOX 1.2**).

BOX 1.2

Using administrative data to analyse incidence of child maltreatment

The two major strategies in analysing agency response to child maltreatment at a national level are via collecting data from frontline workers or using administrative data. As most agencies do collect data on their caseload, using administrative data might seem a cost-effective way to gain insight on the incidence of child maltreatment. However, there is a general lack of uniform data elements not only between different types of agencies but also for the same type of agencies across regions, especially in federally organized countries. Worldwide, only a few examples of nationwide uniform data collection exist, either for CPS or agencies in the health sector (see **CHAPTER II**). In New Zealand, the implementation of a uniform administrative data set was facilitated by a unified protection system for the whole country (*4*). The data set is unique in its daily updates. For more populous and/or federally organized countries, the process of establishing a uniform data set is time-consuming and needs intensive lobbying. In the United States, for example, the process of creating the National Child Abuse and Neglect Data System (NCANDS) was initiated in response to requirements of the federal Child Abuse and Prevention Treatment Act (CAPTA) legislation in 1988 (*5*). It took around a decade to arrive at a close to complete annual report of child maltreatment statistics collected at CPS agencies (*45*). To date, NCANDS is based on a census methodology and incorporates administrative data drawn from CPS responses in each state including both aggregate and case-level data (*4*). All investigations or assessments of alleged maltreatment that receive a disposition in the given year are included in the case-level data collection component (*5*). Information collected includes report sources, demographics and risk factors at the level of the child and the caregivers, maltreatment types, dispositions of the assessment or investigation, and services and placements that result from the investigation. However, even to date, few variables are available across all jurisdictions, and states' varied definitions of maltreatment affect the interpretation of findings. Furthermore, there are issues in reliability of data collection: Changes in trends are relatively likely due to implementation of new data collection software (*46*). The time-consuming process and reliability issues are also known from other national public health data sets (*47, 48*). For countries with a lack of nationally representative data on agency response to child maltreatment, starting with a first wave of a professional survey is often more feasible than trying to implement a public health data set on the topic. A professional survey could subsequently turn out to be an asset in committing agencies and national stakeholders to uniform data collection of administrative data.

1.3.1 Issues in selecting a sample of agencies

Which options a researcher chooses for selecting the sample of agencies – e.g., whether the study focuses on public child protection or includes sentinel agencies such as schools or mental health services – will largely depend on the research questions. An incidence study aiming at national estimates of reports on alleged situations of child maltreatment might embrace a different set of agencies than a study focusing on service response. Although the two levels of sampling at the geographical and the agency level are presented in separate sections, they need to be considered simultaneously: the types of agencies and their scope might differ between provinces or even at a lower administrative level, especially in federally organized countries. For example, in Switzerland, the public CPS differ greatly in type and size. Roughly three types of child welfare agencies providing services can be differentiated: (a) community child and youth centres: in cases of children in need, these services provide nonmandatory support, (b) guardianship services: these organizations strictly provide mandated services, child protection orders enacted by child protection authorities, and (c) polyvalent child and youth centres: these organizations provide both mandated services and nonmandatory support. Many centres are not restricted to supporting only children and youth but also provide social welfare and other services. Sometimes agencies of all three types are found within one canton. Overall, there are currently over 300 child welfare agencies providing services in Switzerland.[13] In comparison, the Canadian Province of Québec, with approximately the same population size of 8 million inhabitants, organizes services to children and youth from 16 youth centres (49).

Sampling at the geographic level. With this report we promote the idea of studying the agency response to child maltreatment at a national level. However, in some situations it might not be feasible to sample agencies in every part of a country: political difficulties between ethnically and/or culturally differing regions might impede nationwide approaches (for example, in Belgium the Flemish region is addressing the issue separately from the Francophone region; see (4)). In a metropolitan centre of a developing country, the child protection system might be much more developed and ready to analyse than in the rest of the same country (**SECTION 1.2**).

If the survey encompasses the whole nation, usually some type of stratification will be applied along administrative units such as provinces or counties that might go along with differences in legislation and policy. It can guarantee that agencies in smaller provinces are included as well and therefore allows for comparing rates between the different regions. Other stratifications might be considered as well, such as linguistically, ethnically or culturally different regions or strata for minority populations to guarantee that enough cases of a particular type will be included in the sample. Besides the strata for provinces and territories, the CIS introduced a separate stratum for Aboriginal agencies to better understand the issue of overrepresentation (36). However, the more clustered your sample is, the less precise the estimates will be (**BOX 1.5**). Whereas agencies in public child protection usually serve a clear cut geographic entity, the catchment area for other branches and agencies may not be as well defined and catchment areas might even overlap. For example, University Children's Hospital Zurich, the oldest and best-known hospital child protection team in Switzerland, serves patients from almost all Swiss cantons; its catchment area overlaps with catchment areas of more recently established child protection teams at other children's hospitals in Switzerland (50). The difficulty of establishing boundaries for a catchment area poses a challenge to calculate rates for agency response to child maltreatment. At the same time, only the use of rates, as

---

[13] A map of agencies in the Swiss child protection system is available at https://www.google.com/maps/d/viewer?mid=zEKhsrVFCQv8.kLeltFTa5kqE.

distinct from the number of incidents, takes into account differences in population size and allow for adequate comparison of maltreatment incidence or service response in different regions or countries.

Sampling at the agency level. Based on the mapping process (**SECTION 1.1**) and the research questions, researchers should decide on what type(s) of agencies to include. Strategies might differ if there is a focus on at-risk groups, on a detailed analysis of maltreated children served by specialized agencies or a broader focus on other types of victimization and developmental risks apart from child maltreatment. Including agencies of the penal sector will provide a focus on responses to perpetrators.

Further issues to consider in agency sampling are size of caseload, the age of children served (such as agencies specializing on infants or adolescents), level of service density (urban vs. rural location), specialization on at-risk population (services for indigenous minorities, migrants, etc.), religiously affiliated services,[14] and population mobility, among others. Sometimes these issues are intertwined with geographic aspects, and agencies might be stratified along these issues.

Once a decision on the types of agencies to include is made, the next step is to establish the sampling frames, which are the comprehensive lists or registries of agencies for the selected types. Lists of public agencies are usually available at the provincial or sometimes even at the national level; some private or semi-private institutions may need licensing by a public institution, and lists may be obtained via licensing bodies or through political lobbying groups for agencies and professions. For other sentinel agencies, lists are more difficult to obtain. In these cases, snowball sampling procedures[15] are an option: often agencies are very familiar with each other in a particular geographic region. Other, less reliable options are telephone book or Internet searches. However, agencies may decline to publish information on these platforms, information might not be up-to-date (agencies may have ceased to exist, changed their name or focus), or names and titles of agencies may differ from the research team's set of keywords.[16] In any case, lists will need re-reviewing for accuracy, duplicated entries and missed groups. To this end, search strategies may also be combined (e.g., combining snowball sampling and Internet searches).

Besides obtaining a list of agencies, researchers also need to implement some screening procedures to determine whether an agency's functions match what the agency's name implies. For example, it might not benefit the study to include agencies that only focus on child maltreatment prevention, and do not receive reports of alleged situations of child maltreatment or provide services to victims. This information is often not automatically apparent from the agency name and has to be checked. Be aware that starting with narrow search terms (e.g. only including agencies that specialize in child maltreatment) could lead you to miss a general social service agency that provides a significant amount of services to maltreated children in a particular region. To avoid the process of compiling agency lists twice it may be advisable to start with broad definitions and then narrow. See **BOX 1.3** for two examples of sampling agencies in the NIS-4 (*10*) and the second wave of the Dutch NPM (*17*).

---

[14] For example, in Toronto, Canada, there are "Children's Aid Societies" for the Jewish and Catholic communities, among others.

[15] Snowball sampling procedures involve identifying and recruiting additional subjects via contact networks of current subjects.

[16] For example, in Germany, many agencies specialized in supporting sexually abused children use symbolic names such as *Wildwasser* ("Wild water") or *Zartbitter* ("Tender and bitter").

BOX 1.3

Agency types and sampling strategies in two professional surveys

The Netherlands: Second National Prevalence Study on Maltreatment (NPM-2010)

Table 1.1. Selected types of agencies and sampling strategy (adapted from (17))

BRANCH: AGENCY TYPE	SAMPLE (n)	SAMPLING STRATEGY
Public child protection		
CPS	15	universe inclusion
Child protection boards[a]	12	regionally stratified random sample
Day and residential care facilities, shelters, housing		
Home-based and center-based child care	77	regionally stratified random sample
Shelters for battered women	48	regionally stratified random sample
Medical agencies		
Well-baby clinics	26	regionally stratified random sample
Emergency departments	6	regionally stratified random sample
General practitioners	131	regionally stratified random sample
Child protection professionals in hospitals[b]	30	regionally stratified random sample
Law enforcement		
Police forces	17	regionally stratified random sample
Schools and school services		
Kindergartens	27	regionally stratified random sample
Primary schools	59	regionally stratified random sample
Secondary schools	28	regionally stratified random sample
Total	**476**	

Notes: a. The investigative branch of public child protection is notified if voluntary means of support are not sufficient and involvement of family court is deemed necessary; b. specialized in the evaluation and response to child maltreatment.

United States: Fourth National Incidence Study on Child Abuse and Neglect (NIS-4)

Table 1.2. Selected types of agencies and sampling strategy (adapted from (10))[a]

BRANCH: AGENCY TYPE	ORIGINAL SAMPLE (n)[b]	SAMPLING STRATEGY
Public child protection		
CPS	126	universe inclusion
Day and residential care facilities, shelters, housing	240	simple random sample
Licensed day care centers	95	simple random sample
Shelters (domestic violence victims, runaway/ homeless youth)	73	universe inclusion
Public housing departments		
Law enforcement		
Sheriff and county police departments	71	universe inclusion in subsample of 62 PSUs[c]
Municipal police agencies	83	PPS to population size in subsample of 62 PSUs
Juvenile probation departments	65	universe inclusion in subsample of 62 PSUs
Medical agencies		
Children's hospitals	40	universe inclusion within 25 miles of NIS-4 PSUs
Short-stay general hospitals	119	PPS[d] to number of beds
Public health departments	114	universe inclusion
Social services and mental health agencies	109	simple random sample from prescreened eligibles
Public Schools	670	PPS to student enrolment
Total	**1 805**	

Notes: a. The sample of agency is based on a sample of 122 counties, selected with probability proportional to size, representing the different regions of the country by degrees of urbanization, crime rates, percentage of households headed by single women, and CPS substantiation rates; b. The original sample of 1805 agencies included 1650 that were in-scope (others were no longer in existence or did not provide direct services to children and families). Of the original in-scope agencies, 1116 participated and 221 of those that refused were replaced, yielding a total of 1220 participating agencies; c. Acronym for Primary sampling unit; d. probability proportionate to size (PPS) is detailed in **BOX 1.4**.

1.3.2   Sampling strategies

Once a list of selected types of agencies has been obtained, there are several models for sampling agencies from these lists or registries. All strategies are based on either random or universe sampling with or without stratification. Convenience samples should be avoided by all means, as they lack representativeness and do not allow for weighting cases to produce national estimates (**BOX 1.5**).

a. **Universe inclusion strategy:** In the Netherlands, for example, public child protection is organized under a unified national legislation. There are 15 CPS agencies (in Dutch: Advies en Meldpunt Kindermishandeling), one in each province and three additional centers in the largest cities (*4*). The NPM research team included all 15 CPS agencies in the first and second wave of data collection (*17*). Of course, there is no limitation to representativeness with a universe inclusion strategy. However, the costs of a study rise with an increasing number of sampled agencies through, for example, an increasing workload for committing the agencies to participation, data entry or data cleaning. Universe inclusion is therefore only feasible with few agencies total for a certain type of agency.

b. **Random sampling strategy:** If universe sampling is not feasible, agencies have to be sampled at random. However, simple random sampling is hardly ever an option because it comes at the cost of a decreased probability of including agencies from small provinces, agencies from areas with low service density, agencies serving minority or indigenous populations, etc. Random sampling will therefore usually be combined with stratification.

c. **Stratification** is applied to avoid the limitations of simple random sampling and to guarantee inclusion of all provinces, a sufficient number of rurally located agencies, etc. However, the number of strata should be limited to avoid the risk of over stratifying: the more different the weights are for the elements in your sample, the less precise your estimates will be.

d. **Probability proportionate to size (PPS):** In this method, each entity in the universe is given a probability of selection that is proportionate to its size, as indexed by some acceptable measure. For instance, in the NIS-4, general stay hospitals were sampled within each primary sampling unit (PSU) with probability proportionate to the number of available beds in the hospital, whereas schools were sampled within each PSU proportionate to their student enrolments. A guide for applying PPS can be found in **BOX 1.4**.

Some surveys combine several strategies (*51*). For instance, in the CIS, agencies were stratified by province or territory, and, in larger provinces, they were further stratified by region and agency size (defined by the number of case openings in a year). In addition, separate strata were developed for Aboriginal agencies. Most sites were selected randomly within their regional strata; agencies in the largest metropolitan areas were sampled with certainty. Due to additional funds provided by provinces, a universe inclusion strategy was applied for non-Aboriginal sites in the provinces of Québec and Saskatchewan. Further examples are described in **BOX 1.3**.

Whereas experts in the field of child protection may lack knowledge on survey methodology, statisticians may lack knowledge on the complexity of a multidisciplinary child protection system. A list of other resources on survey methodology is provided at the end of this chapter. There are only a few examples of nationally representative surveys on agency response to child maltreatment (*10, 11, 17*), but examples are more abundant in health services research (*48, 52–55*).

BOX 1.4

How to apply PPS

In PPS, a list of agencies, administrative or other sampling units is ranked by size, with larger units having an increased likelihood of being included in the sample. In generating a PPS sampling you can follow these instructions: If, for example, a CPS is responsible for the children in a municipality, county or province, the respective administrative unit would be listed in decreasing order of size. Their individual size measures – preferably child population – would be listed next to them, with a third column giving the cumulative count of size, showing how each administrative unit adds to the total population in all units. Divide the number of your target sample size into the total population of administrative units. That gives you your skip number. Drawing a random number between 0 and your skip number gives your starting point. Find your starting point in the cumulative total column. Wherever it falls is the first unit (or agency respectively) you sample. Add the skip number to your starting number. Where it falls is your second sampled unit, and so forth. Often the largest agencies or municipalities will get more than one 'hit' this way, and so they will need to be sampled with certainty. The smallest units will fall below the skip number and have much lower chances of being selected. So combining PPS with stratification is the standard approach to accommodating these issues: The largest units that would be 'hit' 1 or more times in this way are assigned to the study with 'certainty' and have a probability of selection of 1.0. They are each in their own stratum and are removed from the list. The smallest ones should also be removed from the list and aggregated into clusters, so that each municipality or agency cluster meets a minimum combined measure of size. These clusters should now be added to the list, placing them into the list where they belong on the basis of their clustered size.

Further resources on survey methodology

Joint Program in Survey Methodology (JPSM)

The United States-based Joint Program in Survey Methodology (JPSM) is the nation's oldest and largest programme offering graduate training in the principles and practices of survey research. The faculty is drawn among others from Westat, Inc., the organization responsible for managing the NIS cycles.

For more information on short courses, see https://projects.isr.umich.edu/jpsm/

GESIS Summer School in Survey Methodology

The GESIS Summer School is unique in Europe with its focus on survey methodology and data collection.

For more information, see http://www.gesis.org/en/events/gesis-summer-school/

BOX 1.5

Weighting your cases

In any agency survey based on a sample, weights are necessary to calculate national estimates of maltreated children. A researcher designing an agency survey should know what type of information has to be included in the weights to make sure that this information is available. The weights themselves can be calculated retrospectively by a statistician. Two types of information are necessary to calculate weights:

1. Most important, you need to save data on the probability that the agency is included based on the sampling design (design weights). Although it is essential to know the total number of agencies, the probability of inclusion is set deliberately (e.g. 10% of agencies included). To ensure coverage of all provinces, counties or types of agencies, and so on, apply stratification. During the first Swiss agency survey (56), child protection authorities were organized at the municipal level in the German-speaking cantons (provinces). As the median of municipal population in this area was relatively small at this time with around 1000 inhabitants, a first stratum of municipalities with a population of 999 inhabitants or below was created. As these authorities dealt with very few cases of child maltreatment, they were assigned only a small probability of being included. Each subsequent stratum doubled the municipal population of the previous stratum and was given a slightly higher probability of inclusion. All municipalities with a population of 8000 inhabitants and above were completely included (i.e. sampled with certainty), as they represented about half of the population. In this example, municipalities are sampled at different rates, and so they will have different weights in the analysis (as the weight is the inverse of the probability of selection.) It is important to keep in mind that the more different your weights are, the less precise your estimates will be. Furthermore, if you are applying a hierarchical design and sampling from listings of agencies within sampled jurisdictions, your resulting agency sample will be clustered. A clustered sample of agencies will be more homogeneous than a simple random sample of agencies drawn from all jurisdictions, and this has to be taken into account during analyses. Many commonly used statistical software packages will not provide accurate measures of variance for clustered samples (see SECTION 4.5).

2. You further need information on the participation of the sampled agencies to create nonresponse adjustment weights. Unfortunately, nonresponse is virtually unavoidable. By losing part of your sample you are not representing the part of the country that the lost agencies would have represented. To counter your loss you have to 'spread' the weights of the lost agencies across agencies that did participate. A preferable strategy is adding to the weights of those agencies that are most similar to the nonparticipating agencies.

Two caveats have to be considered in applying weights to produce national estimates. One is relatively easily solved: In surveys on agency response to child maltreatment, the samples are likely to cover more than 5% of the population of agencies. The standard errors of estimates about the population are computed from the sample. In doing so, the general assumption is that the sample size is much smaller than the population size. When the sample constitutes more than 5% of the population, statisticians will include a finite population correction (FPC) in the process of computing the standard errors of estimates. This essentially adjusts the variance estimate so that it only applies to the portion of the population that is not in the sample. The second issue is more problematic. Usually, it is not feasible to collect data on agency response to child maltreatment for an entire year; for example, the CIS and NIS use a data reference period of three months (10, 51). In this case, multiplication by four to produce annual estimates would be biased, as it does not take into account potential seasonal variation in caseload or duplication of cases over the course of a calendar year (i.e. the same case reappearing in the agency at different times during the year). Unfortunately, seasonal variation in caseload and case duplication patterns have not been studied extensively and are likely to vary by countries or even by province based on differences in school vacations and religious and other holidays.

Continued →

BOX 1.5 CONTINUED

If public child protection and sentinel agencies are included, seasonal variation and case duplication patterns might also differ between these types of agencies. Pilot studies on seasonal variation or case duplication are often not feasible due to time and funding constraints. In this case, the best option is to not calculate annual estimates but restrict your estimates to the data collection period. Researchers looking for detailed information on annualization factors are referred to the NIS-4. There, CPS agencies provided data on all cases investigated during the course of a full calendar year. The information on source of referral permitted the NIS statisticians to derive unduplicated seasonal variations in the cases encountered in the different sentinel agencies. Appropriate annualization factors were therefore computed for all the different agency sources (35).

2. Case selection

The previous chapter specified the considerations that are important to minimize bias when selecting the agencies to be surveyed in child maltreatment agency-based research. This chapter focuses on selecting case samples from within those agencies; procedures to minimize bias are important to that process as well. Although we have separated sample selection and case selection into two different chapters, planning and decision-making for agency and case selection should be done in a coordinated manner.

In the following sections, we outline several areas of decision-making that will assist in reducing bias in case selection procedures. To start, we discuss the value of process mapping procedures to gather estimates on the number of cases that are coming into the agencies in the sample, their characteristics, and case flow. Second, we discuss the decisions that researchers will need to make about the type of cases that will be sampled, how data will be collected, and time frames for sampling. Third, we discuss different options for sampling including random sampling, stratification, cluster sampling and oversampling. Finally, we review 'unduplication' strategies that may be needed to ensure each case is unique.

2.1   Case process mapping

Case sampling decisions will be aided by having as much information as possible about the sampling frame features. For example, it will be necessary to know as much as possible about the number of cases in the sampling frame. If schools are being sampled, information will be needed on the numbers of children and teachers at each school. If hospitals are being sampled, data on the number of children served by those units over a given period of time (such as annually) is needed. If social services agencies or nongovernmental organizations are being surveyed, the numbers of families and children served will be needed. To inform decisions about sampling unit (incident, child, or family), it will also be helpful to understand how the agency collects information on cases and whether information is crossed-referenced (for example, if two cases come in involving the same child at different times, or different children in the same family, are cases linked by files or file numbers). Additionally, it will also be valuable to obtain at least basic information on the characteristics of the sampling frame. At a minimum, researchers will need to seek out information on the gender, age, and possibly the ethnic and racial distribution[17] of the children in the sampling frame. Decisions about sampling unit, stratification, and unduplication procedures discussed below will be aided by information on the characteristics of the cases.

Next, it will be necessary to map case processes at each of the agencies. How do children enter or come to be seen at the agencies and what percentages of cases are differentially directed at key agency decision points? How do the agencies make decisions about who to

---

[17] Comfort in collecting information on race and ethnicity vary by country (57); however, these data are indispensable for identifying discrepancies in rates of maltreatment or in justice response or service provision across different racial and ethnic groups.

'accept' for services? Are there different levels or different types of services offered based on particular case criteria or characteristics? What are those criteria? See **BOX 2.1** below for an example of case flow of child sexual abuse cases through the United States' criminal justice system. Some agencies will have fairly simple case intake and service structures. Others will be more complicated. For example, in CPS agencies common decision points can include the initial report, case 'acceptance' or investigation procedures, referral, service-delivery, substantiation (for countries in which child protection investigations result in a 'finding' of abuse), follow-up and transfer to family court. For some agencies, case flow decision-making follows standardized and formalized decision-making protocols, based on specified conditions. For other agencies, decisions are less clear-cut and based on ambiguous staff or caseworker procedures. For example, in some social service agencies decisions about what kind of services to provide a family may be made on caseworkers impression about what is needed versus guided by a standardized checklist. Even in the latter case, it will be valuable to collect some information on how cases move through the agency process (see suggestions below). Case flow information is important for a number of sampling decisions, such as decisions about the sampling unit, sampling time frames and sampling procedures. If the purpose of the survey is to collect information about incidence, information about case flow is necessary for deciding how a 'case' will be defined. And if the study intends to track case decision-making and services provided for child victims, case flow data is necessary to inform survey development.

BOX 2.1

An example study of case flow

The following case flow was included in a meta-analytic study looking at the rates at which child sexual abuse cases move through the United States' criminal justice system. The purpose of a study such as this one may be to document rates of case flow through a system, but good mapping procedures conducted in preparation will ensure that the researcher understands the critical case flow points in a system.

Hypothetical case flow of 100 child abuse cases referred for prosecution

Final disposition of 100 hypothetical cases in order of frequency:

Guilty plea	43
Not charged	34
Charge dismissed or transferred	12
Convicted at trial	6
Acquitted at trial	3
Diversion programmes	2
	100

Figure reproduced with permission from (58)

Options for estimating sample frame characteristics and case flow

If the agencies in the sample are unable to provide reliable numbers, it will be necessary to create estimates. This can be done through brief preliminary surveys of a sample of agency staff. This preliminary survey should not take too long or be resource heavy, but the process should have adequate rigour. For example, a randomly selected sample of staff could provide rough numbers of cases seen over a given period of time, and these numbers can then be extrapolated to the cases seen across the agency. Staff can also be surveyed to collect information on the size and characteristics of the sampling frame and on case flow.

Another option for collecting information on case flow, particularly if processes and endpoints are not known, is to randomly select a small sample of newly reported cases and prospectively follow them in a prestudy. You will thus be able to identify processes, decision-making points and statistically calculate the relative risk of different end points.

2.2   Sampling units and data

There are a number of different ways that data can be collected when working with agency data. In part, research questions and the type of agencies included in the study will drive the unit of analysis, the sampling choice, and the method of data collection. But these decisions may also need to be made based on the way that the surveyed agencies define and work with cases, and how they record information about them. Below we discuss the need for researchers conducting agency surveys to make decisions about: (1) the unit of analysis (episode/incident, family, or child), (2) whether data will be collected from case records, via staff informant surveys, or from both, (3) whether data will be collected retrospectively or prospectively, and (4) case time frame issues.

Unit of analysis issues. Researchers need to decide what unit of analysis will be the focus of data collection. Studies may choose to track families (e.g. families with reports of child maltreatment), children who have been reported for maltreatment, incidents of maltreatment, or perpetrators. Decisions about the unit of analysis should mostly be based on study research questions, but may also need to take into account the way that cases are recognized and organized in the agencies being surveyed. A social services agency might record data by family units. Another agency may use child reference identifications. A CPS agency might collect and track data by maltreatment incident or report.

Regardless of the primary unit chosen, when working with the data, it is important to be aware of how units may be nested or may overlap: one perpetrator may target multiple children in the same family, either in one incident or as part of different maltreatment incidents; one child may be maltreated several times, over the course of a year by the same or by multiple perpetrators; and one incident of maltreatment against a child may include many different kinds of maltreatment. It is also important to remember that if you are working with different types of agencies in your study, the structure or even presence of certain data items in one may not correspond to those in another. For example, identifiers for child victims may be easy to extract from CPS agency records, but may be buried or absent in case narratives from law enforcement records that focus on the primary perpetrator.

Ideally, researchers will be able to establish separate but linkable identification numbers for children, perpetrators, and families and identify overlapping units. Such a structure facilitates the calculation of rates and analyses by different units depending on the research question. This kind of data structure can also help to identify duplicated cases (see the section below on unduplication procedures). Depending on how your data is structured, it may be necessary to account for unit of analysis issues in your analyses, particularly if you collect data that is hierarchical (e.g. multiple children or abuse incidents within a family or occurring to a child) (see **CHAPTER 4** for more information on analysing hierarchical data).

Abstracting record data versus conducting staff surveys. Methods of data collection should be decided on as a part of planning case selection. One option is to code or abstract data from case files and records. Another option is to conduct surveys with agency staff about cases that they have seen or agency staff can follow cases forward, depending on whether the study is collecting retrospective or prospective data. It is also possible to combine these approaches in a variety of ways.

There are pros and cons to each type of data collection process, and the choice should be based on research questions and on preliminary information collected about agency data file quality. Case file data abstraction may be less resource intensive than surveying staff directly, but the researcher must consider the quality of the data in the files. There may be limited fields available from which to draw data, missing data may be extensive and uneven, and agencies rarely have checks on the reliability and validity of data entered, either within or across recorders. There also may be restrictions on how much access agencies give to case files. The degree to which agencies store electronic data online and the quality of the organization of files may also impact the researcher's decision on whether case file data abstraction is feasible. If considering case file data abstraction, it will be important to review files at all selected agencies to get a sense of what is collected by the agency and the extensiveness of missing data. It may be possible to supplement missing data with staff interviews, if cases were recent.

The alternative is to survey agency staff about cases. This process provides more control of the type and quality of the data being collected, but researchers will need to put significant time into designing a survey that is understandable to the staff and can be reliably completed, getting staff agreement to participate, training staff in completing the survey, and monitoring data collection if data is going to be collected prospectively. With this strategy, it will also be necessary to make decisions on how agency staff will be sampled, in addition to the cases. A complicated design may require three levels of sampling: cases nested within staff, staff nested within agencies and possibly geographic region as well.

The choosing of the data collection strategy should be made based on a combination of the research questions, the quality of the data that is available from the agencies, and the extent of available resources. There are also supplementary or hybrid options that might work best for particular circumstances: a certain amount of data may be available in case files, and staff caseworkers could be surveyed via short questionnaires to fill in additional needed details.

Retrospective vs. prospective data collection

Data can be collected prospectively or retrospectively. With retrospective data collection, a researcher might pull case information on cases that have come into the agency over the past year or survey professionals on a sample of cases that they have been involved with over the past three months. With prospective data collection, a researcher might plan to collect data from agency staff on cases coming into the agency over a given period of time. **BOX 2.2** provides some examples of how different studies chose to collect data.

Retrospective data collection is typically less expensive, takes less time, and allows the researcher to collect data on cases over a longer period of time. However, if collecting data from case files retrospectively, keep in mind that certain types or categories of cases may have been expunged. Furthermore, collecting data retrospectively from professionals requires a

BOX 2.2

Examples of prospective and retrospective agency data collection

Researchers using agency data to study child victimization have chosen different ways of collecting that data. In the following we provide three examples of how data were collected in these various studies.

The Third National Juvenile Online Victimization Study (N-JOV3). The N-JOV3 study collected information on rates of technology-facilitated child exploitation crimes seen in United States' law enforcement agencies (59). Using a retrospective data collection design, the researchers sent letters to a national sample of law enforcement agencies asking whether they had made any arrests in cases of sexual exploitation of a minor or of child pornography that involved the Internet or new technology in a one-year reference period (January 1, 2009 – December 30, 2009). The researchers then followed up with the agency investigators by telephone and collected in-depth information on the identified arrest cases.

The Fourth National Incidence Study of Child Abuse and Neglect (NIS-4). The NIS-4 study used both retrospective and prospective data collection methods to study child maltreatment rates in the United States (60). Data were captured prospectively from 'sentinel' agency staff (e.g. law enforcement agencies, hospitals, schools, day care centres, mental health agencies) in selected communities, which were asked to code suspected maltreatment over three-month reference periods. Information from CPS agency case records was then collected on investigated children retrospectively for these reference periods, with more frequent retrospective data collection in agencies that purged some case files within a specific time period.

The Canadian Incidence Study of Reported Child Abuse and Neglect-2008 (CIS-2008). This study of the incidence of reported child abuse and neglect in Canada used a prospective data collection process to collect data from child welfare agencies across Canada over a three-month period (61). Case workers were provided with instruments to complete as they worked with cases that were investigated for maltreatment over the study period. Caseworkers were requested to complete the forms when they had finished their written report of the investigation.

reliance on their memory, which means there may be some error. The level of error will depend on the design and the nature of the agency, the staff persons' roles, and their caseloads. The more cases per professional, the more they will have to rely on case files to supplement what they remember. Relying on memory may also introduce some systematic biases. Caseworkers may do a better job at remembering cases with particular types of maltreatment or may remember more details.

Prospective data collection allows the researcher to have more control and allows for collecting data systematically on variables that are not typically documented in case files. It may be more time consuming to collect data prospectively, particularly if outcomes of interest occur months or even years after intake. Additionally, if data are going to be collected prospectively from caseworkers, then fairly extensive training procedures are needed. There is also the possibility that the researcher might influence the actual activity with the case or case processing through the research itself.

Ultimately, decisions on how data will be collected, similar to decisions on the source of the data, will depend on research questions, cost considerations, recent and upcoming changes in agency practices and policies and the time frame for the study. The more information that researchers can collect about the involved agencies, the staff, and the nature of the cases, the more successful they will be in making sampling decisions and interpreting study results.

Case time frame decisions

Finally, regardless of how data are collected, researchers will need to consider time frame decisions. If data are going to be collected retrospectively from case files or by professional survey, how far back will cases be sampled? If prospective data will be collected, decisions will have to be made on the time period for enrolling new cases and on how long cases will be followed. The considerations involved in time frame decisions will be influenced by the types of data collected. If data are collected retrospectively by professional surveys, and respondents are going to have to rely on memory a fair amount, then the researcher will have to be careful not to extend the time frame too far back. One issue that can also occur with relying on memory is telescoping (*62*). In telescoping, study respondents tend to remember salient distant events as happening more recently. This will affect the survey if researchers ask professionals, for example, to judge, based on memory, the number of cases seen in a given amount of time, case dates, durations, and frequencies. Finally, researchers will also need to keep in mind seasonal variation in case intake and flow and how that may affect time frame decisions. This is less of a problem if cases are sampled evenly over the duration of a year or multiple years, but it can affect how representative cases are that are collected over a shorter period of time. Cost and resources and project budget also affect decisions on time frame, particularly in the case of prospective data collection.

2.3 Sampling procedures

Once the nature of the agency cases and procedures are well-known to the researcher, and in conjunction with decisions about how data will be collected, from what sources, and over what time period, the researcher must also make decisions on procedures for sampling cases. A good sampling process is critical to minimizing bias and increasing the chance that the sample is representative of the universe of cases of interest. There are entire textbooks written about sampling strategies (*63–65*). Here we provide researchers with a brief overview of the methods and strategies that are often used to minimize bias.

Avoiding biased sampling

The goal of conducting research is to understand something about the experiences of a larger group of individuals. In our case, researchers are interested in understanding rates of children's exposure to violence as identified by particular agencies or professionals, or the protective and service responses provided to these youth and their families. The research population is the larger group to which the researcher hopes their sample will generalize, for example, young people under 18 years in a given geographic area. The sampling frame, however, includes only those cases that have a chance of being selected into the study. For example, a sampling frame might be all young people under 18 years who were seen at hospitals in the geographic region of interest in the year time frame of the study. **FIGURE 2.1** is an aid to visualizing this example. Sampling procedures that the researcher chooses will determine who in the sampling frame will actually be included in the sample. The more rigorous the sampling process is, the more accurately the researcher can generalize findings back to the sampling frame.

Sampling bias occurs when cases are chosen for inclusion in the sample in such a way that some cases are systematically more or less likely to be included than others. There are different kinds of sampling biases (*66*), but we will describe two in more detail: selection and exclusion bias. Selection bias occurs when sampling procedures result in a situation in which certain types of cases are more likely to be included in a study than others. This can bias the results of the study, because study findings may be misinterpreted as representative of the

Fig. 2.1 Relationship between the research population, sampling frame, and sample

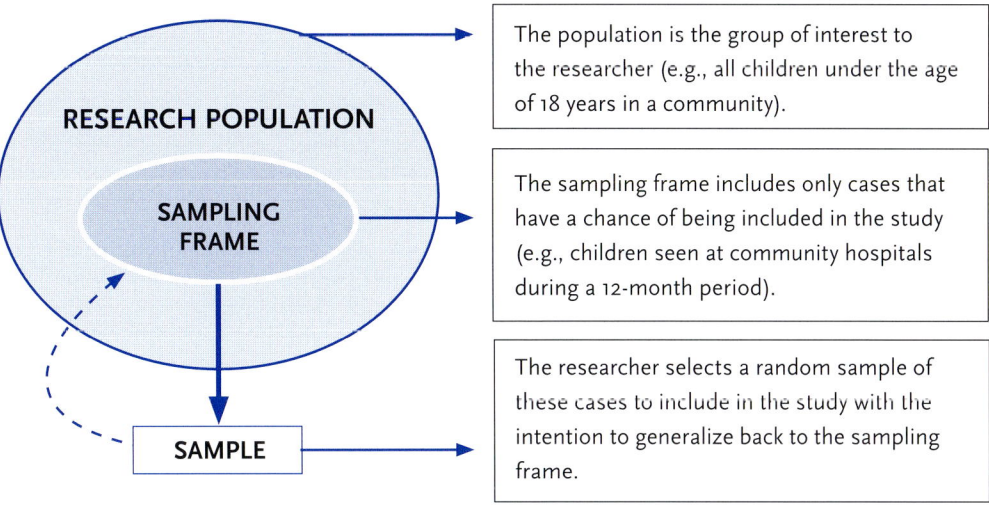

population, or even a particular sampling frame, when they are not. An example of selection bias might be if caseworkers were allowed to select cases for inclusion in the study. Cases that were more memorable, such as those that were very dramatic or those that showcased successful work by the agency, might be more likely to be included than others. Exclusion bias describes a situation in which some cases are more likely to be excluded from the sample because of particular characteristics. For example, if an agency did not want to have the researcher include cases that were controversial, say because of the case outcome, this would introduce systematic bias into the sample.

Methods of probability sampling

Probability sampling is a way to make sure that the sample is as unbiased as possible. Probability sampling means that a random selection process is used to select cases into the sample that does not rely on convenience samples or researcher, caseworker, professional or agency choice in deciding which cases will be included in the study and which will not.

The easiest way to sample with probability is to use simple or systematic random sampling. In this kind of sampling, each case in the sampling frame has the exact same probability as any other of being selected for the study. An example would be selecting cases across some specific interval, such as selecting every tenth case in the file. Or, if all case file numbers are available and can be represented in a computer file, most spreadsheets offer a way to select cases randomly.

Sometimes, however, there is an interest not just in representing the overall sample frame, but doing so in a way that allows the researcher to study particular types or subgroups of cases. In this case, the researcher will likely want to use a stratified random sampling process. Here, the sampling frame is divided by homogenous subgroups of interest, for example, by gender, age, race and ethnicity, or even type of maltreatment report. Random sampling is then done separately from among each group. Stratified samples can be selected proportionately, so that the percentage of subgroup cases in the sample matches the percentage in the sampling frame. Or an oversampling process can be used, so that adequate numbers of a smaller subgroup of interest are achieved. Although proportionally the sample will now be different from the sampling frame and final estimates will be less precise because the cases will have different final weights, sampling weights will allow the sample to represent the universe of cases that is the focus of the research.

Since these guidelines are specifically targeted at researchers who will be collecting agency data, it is important to keep in mind that the methods are actually likely to involve multiple stages of sampling, in which the final cases are clustered by the elements at the earlier stages of sampling. Cases may be randomly sampled from within agencies, and agencies from within particular geographic regions. It may also be that the researcher will be sampling cases from the caseloads of particular professionals that have themselves been sampled from within agencies. All of these layers require more sophisticated sampling and weighting strategies.

It may also be that researchers will want to choose a different sampling strategy across clusters. For example, consider a situation where medical professionals in a hospital will be surveyed about youth cases that they will see over the next three months. To reduce the measurement burden, the researcher may want to randomly sample cases from paediatricians' caseload, because they see so many, but to include all youth cases for other physicians at the hospital, who may have fewer cases meeting inclusion criteria. The N-JOV3 study described in **BOX 2.2** above used this kind of sampling process: for law enforcement agencies that reported from one to three arrests involving technology-facilitated child exploitation, follow-up telephone interviews were conducted for all cases; when agencies reported four or more arrests, a hierarchical decision was made to conduct interviews for all cases in which there was an identified victim and to randomly select cases with no identified victim (e.g. child pornography cases).

2.4   Dealing with duplication issues

One of the final issues that the researcher will have to deal with relevant to case sampling procedures is duplication concerns. Whether the intention is to study rates of child maltreatment identified by the agency, or to study typical case process and service delivery, duplicated cases increase error because estimation procedures assume that each case is unique. Duplication can occur in a number of different ways: the same episode or case can be picked up across multiple agencies in the study; there can be multiple incidents per child; and there can be multiple incidents, multiple victims, and multiple perpetrators per family.

Some of the decisions about identifying duplicate cases will be driven by the research question, the type of data collection, and the organization of the agency records (e.g. incident-based, child-based, offender-based, or family-based). The case mapping process discussed above in this section will help researchers prepare for potential problems with duplication ahead of time. Ideally, the agencies will have a way to help identify duplicated cases (e.g. assigning identification numbers to each family, and linking them with different identification numbers assigned to each child), but this is often not the case. It is even more complex to identify duplicate cases across agencies. Regardless, it is necessary for researchers to think carefully through options for identifying duplicated cases.

The best process for identifying duplicate cases is for the researcher to include as many unique identifiers in the database as possible. Sometimes this will be limited by how much identifying information is available from files. Family members' names and dates of birth and agency identification numbers are good options. Addresses can also be used. If privacy protections or human subject committee requirements limit the identifying information that can be delivered to the researcher, one option is to have the agency keep a file of identifiers linked with research identification numbers, while the researcher uses a de-identified research database for data analysis. Case duplication can be checked manually, although this is labour-intensive depending on the size of the sample. Computer applications are available to researchers to check duplication, including software developed by the United States' Centers for Disease Control and Prevention (CDC). **BOX 2.3** provides an example of how the NIS-4 identified duplicated cases.

BOX 2.3

Example of an unduplication process: Fourth National Incidence Study (NIS-4)

Because one of the goals of the NIS-4 was to provide estimates of the number of maltreated children, it was important to develop a way to identify and eliminate duplicates – cases that appeared in sentinel reports or surveys twice or more during the data collection period. The NIS-4 researchers devised a detailed unduplication process.

The NIS-4 unduplication process (60) matched candidate pairs on eight key data items: first name, last name initial, gender, date of birth, age, ethnicity/race, city of residence, number of children in family. Then, staff manually identified possible duplicates by sorting computerized files of reports in nine participating counties. These candidate pairs were then used to set the parameters of a probability-based matching software and to adjust an unduplication algorithm used in NIS-3 to identify probable matches in the remaining study counties. Finally, staff then manually reviewed the pairs identified by the software and algorithm to determine if they were true duplicates (about 40% of candidate pairs were identified as true duplicates). Reliability procedures were implemented by obtaining a second blind decision on all candidate pairs in the nine counties where duplicates were identified manually and in 10% of cases for the remaining counties.

For some cases from CPS agencies there was no additional information beyond the key demographic items on which to judge whether a candidate pair was a true duplicate or not. Statisticians therefore used the information on true duplicates identified in the process described above to further adjust the probability-based matching software. The software was then used to generate true duplicate pairs with the child protection cases that had limited data.

The final unduplication step for the NIS-4 was to select a single record from the duplicates to represent the child in the final database. The choice of which record to use was based on a hierarchical decision process stemming from study research questions. For example, preference was given to records indicating countable maltreatment, complete demographic information, and sentinel sources higher in the NIS hierarchy. Lastly. the child's statistical weights were adjusted to account for the multiple chances that the child had of entering the study.

3. Definitions, variables and coding

3.1 Important processes for researchers

The specification of variable definitions and coding procedures should start early in the research design and planning phase. Definitions can be pretested and refined while selecting the agency sample, mapping agency case flow, and getting to know how the involved agencies and professionals organize their information on cases. The coding process should then be revisited and tested continually during data collection to check on reliability and validity. Below are some key tips for researchers throughout this process. The chapter is complemented by boxes on selecting variables, caveats associated with this process, and an extended section on the core elements of maltreatment definitions.

3.1.1 Draw on the definitional work that others have done

A great deal of definition development and coding work has already been done by experienced child maltreatment researchers, including many who have designed surveys or procedures specifically to collect data from agencies and professionals. They have learned from and corrected design and coding problems, and they have identified fields and definitional structures that provide interpretable and meaningful data. So it makes sense to build on this trial and error work that has already taken place. Although it is likely that adaptations will be necessary to fit the circumstances of any new study (e.g. due to differences in agency type, case file structure, and local or agency culture), researchers can avoid numerous problems down the road by building on prior definitional work. Start by collecting a sizeable number of existing data collection measures and review the fields that they have in common, how definitions are worded, and how they structure the coding.

3.1.2 Include variables/fields found useful by others

There are numerous fields that have been found useful by researchers conducting a wide range of maltreatment research studies, even in different communities and countries. Commonly collected variables include, for example, the child's age, the type of maltreatment alleged (or reported or confirmed), the perpetrator's relationship to the child and whether the child is under the care of the state. For more discussion on typical variables included in research on child maltreatment, see **BOXES 3.1, 3.2 AND 3.3** below and review some of the resources provided at the end of this chapter. Because so many researchers find the same variables important in analysing and understanding child maltreatment case data, researchers conducting new studies should consider including as many of those variables as possible. This will ensure that nothing potentially important is inadvertently overlooked. It will also increase the likelihood that the research findings can be analysed in ways that will answer questions that stakeholders may have, and findings can be compared to parallel research being conducted in other geographical locations.

BOX 3.1

Definitions of variables used in sampling cases

Compared to population surveys aiming at collecting data on the prevalence of child maltreatment within the last year or a lifetime, the criteria for sampling cases in studies on agency response to child maltreatment are primarily driven by the processes of the agencies. Most previous agency surveys have sampled cases that had been reported to the agencies within a three-month period (10, 16, 17, 51). The analyses of United States administrative data on child protection are conducted annually (45, 67); other countries such as New Zealand or the Republic of Korea have central child welfare data bases that are updated daily (4, 26, 27). The lag between onset of maltreatment and a report to CPS or other agencies might differ remarkably within the caseload. While the studies cited above focused on cases reported for maltreatment, depending on the research question, investigators might also consider sampling across other decision points on the continuum of professional care, for example cases that are referred for assessment, cases that receive a particular assessment classification, cases in which maltreatment is substantiated, cases that are referred for services or child removal, and cases where services are terminated.

Defining children's age categories for your sample will be intertwined with sampling certain types of agencies. Some agencies, particularly public child protection agencies, serve the whole range from infants to the country's age of majority or even beyond. Other (sentinel) agencies focus on infants and toddlers (e.g. Dutch well-baby clinics, American Head Start services), school-aged children (e.g. school social workers, school psychological services) or a juvenile population. Depending on the selection of agencies, certain age groups might be overrepresented in your sample.

Budgetary reasons as well as specific research aims might lead researchers to focus on populations of interest instead of the child welfare population in general. Samples may be defined as populations at risk (Aboriginal populations or other minorities, children with disabilities, refugees, etc.), through their relationship to the state (children with a child protective order, etc.) or their living arrangement (single caregiver households, kinship or foster care, etc.).

Acceptance of questionnaires by caseworkers may increase if you add a few open questions that allow them to expand on their thoughts (68). Furthermore, this kind of question can be useful in adding contextual understanding or illustrative examples. Be cautious, however, about relying on too many open-ended questions. Systematically coding these kind of responses is time-consuming and can provide less consistent or generalizable information than questions with structured response options.

3.1.3 Use specific and detailed definitions

Researchers have found it important to use concrete and specific descriptions of maltreatment types, evidence and harm. Socially constructed labels, vague and general terms should be avoided. This will increase the reliability of the data – the likelihood that similar incidents will be coded the same way across coders and by the same coder over time. Definitional specificity also increases the ability to replicate data collection over time, to account for definitional additions or changes in the future, and to compare with other research.

Others have found it useful to begin with a broad definition followed by specific indicators. For example, the United States' Centers for Disease Prevention and Control report, Child maltreatment surveillance: uniform definitions for public health and recommended data elements, defines child physical abuse as:

> Physical abuse is the intentional use of physical force against a child that results in or has the potential to result in physical injury. Physical abuse includes physical acts ranging from those which do not leave a physical mark on the child to those which cause permanent disability, disfigurement, or death. Physical abuse can result from discipline or physical punishment and is coded regardless of the caregiver's intent to harm or injure the child. (69)

Some data collection tools query coders or respondents about specific acts that are defined as falling within the definition of physical abuse or another type of maltreatment (10, 11). For example, codes for "punch, kick, or bite" or "hit with object" would identify a case of physical abuse (11).

To further increase reliability, measurement should be grounded as much as possible using comparable and clear-cut anchors. For example, coding for the presence of child maltreatment often includes measurement of injury. This is an important aspect of understanding abuse severity, but it can be difficult to code as many professionals in child protection do not routinely assess injuries. Using specific language to either denote specific types of injuries or to define in detail a level of injury can improve reliability.

The goal with definitional specificity is not only to be able to provide general summaries, but also to be able to carve up the data in ways that will be meaningful to various stakeholders and researchers. For example, many researchers will want to be able to calculate data in a way that parallels statutory definitions (including (70)). This may be of particular interest, for example, to child maltreatment agencies and policy-makers. But it will likely also be important to be able to provide more generalized information on maltreatment cases in a way that is not limited by those definitions. Asking general questions with well-anchored definitions to begin with, and then following up with more specific targeted questions will help produce findings that will be of interest to a variety of different groups. An extended discussion of issues related to selecting a child maltreatment definition for your study can be found at the end of this chapter.

3.1.4   *Pretest and adapt definitional language to local situations*

Beginning with definitions created by others is a good place to start; however, it will be important to make sure the definitions are consistent with local language, culture and conditions. Will coders have the information needed to use and apply the definitions? Does the language make sense, given how respondents think about and collect information on cases? If not, definitional language and perhaps the questionnaire items themselves may need to be adapted. For information specific to case processing, flow and services, it will be particularly important to make sure that the language is relevant to the local agency and community systems.

3.1.5   *Use training, pretesting and ongoing monitoring to increase reliability*

Even with well-constructed and specific definitions, it will be important to build in a number of procedures to ensure that the definitions are clear to coders or agency staff respondents. Training for those responsible for data collection will be necessary to obtain consistent, reliable and valid data. If agency records are being coded, coding procedures will need to be developed and tested. If agency staff are being asked to collect data prospectively, they will have to be trained to understand and use the study definitions. Even if agency professionals are being surveyed retrospectively, it will be important to pretest survey questions and definitions to identify problems. Focus groups can be held with respondents or agency staff to gather feedback on the definitions and data collection instruments.

BOX 3.2

Defining and coding demographics, risk factors and service provision

In coding risk and protective factors or data on the maltreatment event, researchers have to consider that information collected does not necessarily depict the child's or family's entire current situation, but merely captures information that the professional has noted. A caregiver's mental health issue (or any other problem) might potentially go unnoticed.

The following paragraphs present notes on miscellaneous variables. For more information, we refer the reader to the list of additional resources at the end of this chapter.

Economic hardship

There is a wide variety of techniques to operationalize economic hardship, from crude proxies to more sophisticated approaches (71). Many studies operationalize economic hardship through household and social characteristics. The CIS, for example, includes home status as measured by the categories of home ownership, rent, lives in public housing, lives in band housing,[a] stays in a hotel or shelter, or other (11). Other forms found across the literature are indicators of economic resources, neighbourhood characteristics or macroeconomic conditions such as recession and high unemployment (71). A detailed measure of economic hardship in families involved in the child protection system will be difficult to establish, however, as information is often not readily accessible by child welfare professionals. In fact, poverty indicators are among the variables most frequently missing in previous agency surveys (71). A strategy to increase validity is approximating poverty by several indicators in your survey. Further recommendations include the application of poverty thresholds of generally widely studied metrics established by a country's statistical office.

Ethno-racial variables

Agency surveys from Canada and the United States have used variables combining ethnic and racial categories. NIS-4, for example, uses six categories in its ethno-racial variable: (1) American Indian or Alaskan Native, (2) Asian or Pacific Islander, (3) Black, not of Hispanic origin, (4) Hispanic, (5) White, not of Hispanic origin, (6) Other. However, ethno-racial categories are subject to – sometimes heated – political and academic debates. France and perhaps other countries have laws banning professionals and administrators from directly or indirectly collecting data on a client's ethnicity and race (72).

Services

The agency mapping process, described in SECTION 1.1, is essential not only for adequately coding the institutional sources of reporting to CPS or other agencies, but also for the referral to other agencies once a child has been investigated or assessed by a certain agency. Detailed categories for types of services provided will depend on national (and provincial) legislation and professional policy. Researchers aiming at international comparison of types of services might include categories such as in-home counselling, parent support groups, psychosocial counselling, psychiatric or psychological services, medical or dental services, drug or alcohol counselling, shelter services, welfare or social assistance, special education placement, child or day care, recreational services, etc.) (11). We recommend enlarging the evidence on different types of child welfare services, as research on services other than out-of-home placement is still scarce (73).

....
[a] Aboriginal housing built, managed, and owned by the band.

Researchers should use reliability procedures to ensure consistency among coders when information is being abstracted from case files. There are resources available that explain these procedures in detail, but the process at its most basic involves having two coders code a certain percentage of the same files or cases separately and then calculating the agreement. Ideally, this process should happen early in the development of definitions and data collection tools, so that they can be edited and refined to improve reliability to a point that is acceptable. A similar process could also be developed to check the reliability of professional surveys. For example, vignettes might be provided to respondents to see how they respond to or report on hypothetical cases.

As much as possible, efforts to establish and pretest clear, specific definitions and coding procedures should be conducted prior to the data collection phase. Changing definitions during the study will result in different and sometimes noncomparable data sets. However, it is important to make sure that research staff or agency staff who are collecting data or responding to surveys have the ability to ask questions throughout data collection. Contact professionals actively and regularly to remind them about the study and to answer any questions that they may have. Agency staff should also have contact information for the research team for questions about completing data forms, and the researchers should be easily accessible. If resources allow, it can be particularly valuable to have on-site coordinators to help data collectors with translation and to answer questions. Conduct regular check-in meetings with research staff who are doing any coding, so that they can ask questions and review problems.

Finally, thoroughly document all the processes and decisions made in creating variables and definitions, including pretesting, editing and reliability checks.

3.1.6   *Take care to interpret findings with consideration of their limits*

Following data collection, if it is not clear how certain fields or questions were interpreted by respondents, follow-up focus groups or testing (e.g. with case vignettes) can be used to gather information on interpretation. With these data and other information collected on agency processes, it will be important to interpret the findings very carefully. Consider, as an example, that research on child maltreatment often collects information about risk: For example, whether domestic violence is occurring in the household, or whether one of the caregivers has mental illness diagnoses or has alcohol or drug abuse problems. It is important to keep in mind when interpreting and writing about the findings that such data will typically represent information on whether the risk was noted or not, either in the case file or by the field worker. If the risk is noted, it is likely present. However, if the risk is not noted, the judgement is less reliable. It will be important to make sure that interpretations of the findings reflect an accurate understanding of the data. Information that is collected in the preparation stages of the study on agency procedures will help to gauge how consistently and reliably the variables of interest are screened. If information is collected on a key risk factor as a part of systematic intake procedures, using a standardized screening protocol, then more confidence can be placed in the meaning of that data. However, in many agencies, such risk factors are noted in files only if they happen to come up in referral or via interview. Furthermore, the selection of risk variables collected in different agency surveys varies with the focus of a research team.

BOX 3.3

Variables related to the agency's administrative unit

Even though it is generally accepted that child welfare decisions are driven not only by child and family characteristics, but also by agency policies, provincial legislation, decision-makers' experience, etc. (74), research on the impact of factors at these secondary levels is still scarce, although emerging (73, 75–77). If a public agency is responsible for a specific administrative unit (district, county, province, etc.), there is generally census data available that might be merged into the data set at the level of the agency or the administrative unit, respectively. The advantage of census data on child population, prevalence of unemployment, living costs, etc. is that the data already come with a definition and operationalization and enrich the data set with information at the macro level. Furthermore, national statistical offices often provide a standardized measurement of urban and rural areas (see, for example, http://www.ers.usda.gov/data-products/rural-urban-continuum-codes/documentation.aspx).

3.2 Issues in defining child maltreatment

Unfortunately, consensus among practitioners and researchers on shared definitions of child maltreatment is lacking. The different generic terms in use – child maltreatment or child abuse and neglect, among others – indicate the definitional variety. Differences in epidemiological and practice-oriented or statutory definitions are associated with different goals. Epidemiologists are mostly interested in linking the frequency of phenomena with preceding causes or subsequent consequences, while practitioners are concerned with providing scarce resources to children at risk. The threshold for intervention is dependent on the culturally and time-variant societal and legal context (78, 79). An epidemiologist might well consider a single act of belittling a child a potentially harmful event of psychological maltreatment, but frontline staff might only acknowledge such an occurrence as maltreatment if it presents as a chronic pattern (80).

Definitions vary not only between practice and research, but also between the different disciplines (i.e. social work, psychology, sociology, medicine) interested in contributing knowledge to improve support for victimized children. Among debated issues is whether a definition of child maltreatment should be based on acts of perpetrators, on the consequences for the child, on the context of the event, or a combination of these elements. Further divergence arises on the inclusion of actual or potential harm (78, 79). The definitions are also subject to changes over time. In the future, not only may societal consensus evolve regarding what defines optimal child rearing but also knowledge may change on what kinds of behaviour or experience are harmful or not harmful for children (81). However, the choice of a maltreatment definition will ultimately depend on the research questions (e.g. if the investigators want to make international comparisons or aim at results on how well the cases match statutory definitions).

Most maltreatment definitions include acts of commission and omission, and the subdivision into the categories of psychological maltreatment, neglect, physical maltreatment and sexual abuse is widely accepted. Whereas codes for physical maltreatment and sexual abuse are generally evident for professionals, there is more ambiguity around definitions of psychological maltreatment and neglect. With imprecise operationalization of definitions, the boundaries between, for example, certain emotional acts of omission and commission tend to blur, and reliability of coding therefore decreases. For more definitional and operational clarity, recent definitional approaches of neglect tend to subdivide the phenomena into failure to provide

Fig. 3.1 Maltreatment codes of the CIS-2008 child maltreatment assessment form (11)

MALTREATMENT CODES				
PHYSICAL ABUSE	SEXUAL ABUSE	NEGLECT	EMOTIONAL MALTREATMENT	EXPOSURE TO INTIMATE PARTNER VIOLENCE
1 Shake, push, grab or throw	7 Penetration	16 Failure to supervise: physical harm	24 Terrorizing or threat of violence	29 Direct witness to physical violence
2 Hit with hand	8 Attempted penetration	17 Failure to supervise: sexual abuse	25 Verbal abuse or belittling	30 Indirect exposure to physical violence
3 Punch, kick or bite	9 Oral sex	18 Permitting criminal behaviour	26 Isolation / confinement	31 Exposure to emotional violence
4 Hit with object	10 Fondling	19 Physical neglect	27 Inadequate nurturing or affection	-------------------------
5 Choking, poisoning, stabbing	11 Sex talk or images	20 Medical neglect (includes dental)	28 Exploiting or corrupting behaviour	32 Exposure to non-partner physical violence
6 Other physical abuse	12 Voyeurism	21 Failure to provide psychological treatment		
	13 Exhibitionism	22 Abandonment		
	14 Exploitation	23 Educational neglect		
	15 Other sexual abuse			

basic needs and failure to adequately supervise (69, 82). Researchers might be interested not only in coding the different forms of child maltreatment, but also in more accurately capturing the event/situation of child maltreatment – whether the child's physical, emotional or educational needs had been neglected or the child had been hit with the perpetrator's hand or an object. Strategies of implementing this approach have used codes for the different forms of maltreatment and descriptive subcodes for capturing the concrete nature of the maltreatment (see **FIG. 3.1**).

Various definitions of ('traditional') child maltreatment subtypes overlap with definitions of other forms of child victimization (e.g. child labour, bullying). This is most manifest for events of exposure to intimate partner violence. Whereas many consider a child's exposure to intimate partner violence a separate form of child victimization, others code events of exposure to intimate partner violence as a form of psychological maltreatment. For many studies it will make sense to cover exposure to intimate partner violence separately, as these situations are frequent in the caseload of child protection agencies (83). Other forms of endangerment to a child's development might also be included based on their prevalence in the agency's caseload or statutory definitions. For example, CPS in the Canadian province of Québec applies the code of behavioural problems as a separate code beside four categories of child maltreatment[18] (49).

....

[18] Social workers can therefore choose between five different options to code the situations that they are confronted with.

Agencies in the child protection system are regularly confronted with events below the threshold of maltreatment that are nonetheless a potential danger for the optimal development of the child. These events or situations are sometimes labelled: risk for future maltreatment. It may be of value to include this or similar categories in data collection, as long as they are concretely defined. Thresholds distinguishing undesirable child rearing practices from child maltreatment vary between agencies and professionals (74) and as far as risk factors are concerned, the category of risk for future maltreatment is difficult to differentiate from actual maltreatment categories. In epidemiological studies from Canada and the United States, children labelled as being at risk of future maltreatment presented with as many household and caregiver risks as investigated cases that were substantiated (84). Therefore, by excluding the category of risk for future maltreatment from your surveys you might potentially exclude a substantial number of cases with unidentified events of maltreatment.

Child maltreatment events and situations can vary along several dimensions – severity and chronicity, for instance. The operationalization of chronicity of child maltreatment in studies on agency response to child maltreatment is tricky. First, the concept covers several aspects; besides the first occurrence of a maltreatment incident and the number of maltreatment incidents (i.e. frequency), patterns of chronicity are further characterized in terms of how many of a child's calendar or developmental periods include maltreatment (i.e. the extent of it) and whether or not there are gaps in the pattern of maltreatment (i.e. continuity) (80). The age of onset of a neglect situation, its frequency and its continuity are especially difficult to reliably substantiate and code. Onset and frequency are therefore sometimes measured by proxies such as first report to CPS or frequency of re-reports (80, 85). An alternative definition of chronicity comprises five ordinal categories ranging from (1) situational, (2) limited episodic, (3) limited continuous, (4) extended episodic, to (5) extended continuous (80). In isolation from other dimensions of maltreatment such as type or severity, different definitions of chronicity have been found to account for different aspects of the outcomes of interest (80).

The assessment of maltreatment severity not only depends on cultural background but also will likely vary between agencies and professionals. Reliability will improve if you are able to establish an operationalization of categories that is based on accessible and manifest information. The following example of classifying the severity of physical maltreatment in ordinal categories is from the Modified Maltreatment Classification System (MMCS) used in the LONGSCAN studies (82):

1 = Dangerous acts, but no marks indicated

2 = Minor marks (small scratches, cuts or bruises)

3 = Numerous or non-minor mark(s)

4 = Medical/emergency treatment; hospitalized less than 24 hours

5 = Hospitalized more than 24 hours

6 = Permanent disability/scarring/disfigurement/fatality

Ordinal severity ratings per maltreatment type can be used or, in the case of multiple maltreatment experiences, ratings can be combined to create total or mean severity scores. However, Litrownik et al. (86) found that an operational definition of maltreatment severity that provides the most predictive power for child developmental outcomes would preserve a severity rating within each type of maltreatment rather than combining the information on severity in an overall mean or maximum severity score. The limitations of measuring (physical) harm as a proxy for severity are, first, the correlational relation between severity and harm – not every severe maltreatment incident necessarily leads to substantial harm. Second, even physical harm often lags behind the actual maltreatment event or situation; the lag may therefore lead to an underestimation of severity (87–90).

Information about the perpetrator(s) is an additional area of data collection that provides important information on child maltreatment. While definitions of neglect and physical or psychological maltreatment generally refer to caregiver-perpetrated acts, definitions of child sexual abuse often include both stranger- and peer-perpetrated sexual violence towards children. This definitional variability is responsible for mixed results on risk factors for child sexual abuse, as risk factors and outcomes differ for children sexually victimized by caregivers, peers or strangers (91, 92). To increase the accuracy of statistical comparisons, while at the same time responding to those who may define maltreatment in different ways, researchers may want to collect data on cases broadly defined (e.g., including peer and stranger perpetrated cases), and narrow for particular research purposes.

Although different definitions might be preferred depending on the research questions, operationalization of definitional elements is essential for any survey or analysis of administrative data. An example of successful operationalization including state of the art evidence on child maltreatment research is the approach of the United States' Centers for Disease Control and Prevention (69). It is built on consensus among disciplines from medicine to social work. Building on child maltreatment definitions of previous studies is a helpful strategy. However, keep in mind that definitions need to make sense to field workers to avoid biases: If research definitions are too different from the definitions used in practice, data collection might be biased. The acceptance of definitions likely varies between different professions. The gap between research definitions and (formal or informal) definitions-in-use is often the widest for definitions of neglect (93). A strategy of building acceptance for your study might be to include practitioners in the development or adaptation of definitions. See **SECTION 5.1** for a more extensive discussion of research–practice partnerships.

Further resources

Previous agency surveys and analyses of administrative data (see **CHAPTER 2** for further resources)

Maltreatment definitions and operationalization

Child maltreatment surveillance: uniform definitions for public health and recommended data elements (69)
The United States' Centers for Disease Prevention and Control (CDC) provide individuals and organizations in the public health community with uniform definitions and recommended data elements on child maltreatment and its associated terms.
http://www.cdc.gov/ViolencePrevention/pub/CMP-Surveillance.html

Modified Maltreatment Coding System (MMCS)
The instrument applied in the LONGSCAN studies is available at http://www.unc.edu/depts/sph/longscan/pages/maltx/mmcs/LONGSCAN%20MMCS%20Coding.pdf

Further documents related to maltreatment coding are available at http://www.unc.edu/depts/sph/longscan/pages/maltx/index.htm

Risk and protective factors

Reviews of risk factors for family violence (see "Risk Factors for Family Violence: Introduction to the Special Series" by Heyman and Smith Slep (94))

Eight articles in the special series of the journal Aggression and Violent Behavior review the strength of risk factors for family violence; they provide "a convenient summary from which to identify the strengths and weaknesses of the current risk and protective factor knowledge" (94). Of special interest are the reviews on neglect (95), psychological maltreatment (96), sexual abuse (91) and physical maltreatment (97).

Outcomes

International Society for Child Indicators (ISCI)
The ISCI webpage connects researchers with further resources on measuring child outcomes. See http://isci.chapinhall.org/

4. Statistical modelling

The major goal of nationally representative agency surveys tends to be descriptive statistics on the magnitude of reported child maltreatment incidents. The data may, however, also be used to address hypotheses that require the researcher to rely partially on statistical modelling. Unfortunately, many social scientists fear that statistical modelling is too complex for them to apply. Statisticians, on the other hand, sometimes have trouble understanding the aims of the intended analyses and might apply inappropriate models. This chapter therefore introduces important concepts and terms associated with statistical modelling and the difficulties typically encountered. The aim is to link novices on the topic with useful resources or to facilitate their communication with statisticians, and does not replace a textbook or training.

Note that many statistical models may be parameterized quite differently using either a 'traditional' general linear model (GLM) approach or other techniques, such as structural equation modelling (SEM). For an introduction to SEM and its advantage of modelling relationships between latent and manifest (or other latent) constructs, see Kline (98). Other techniques to model latent constructs may also prove relevant to your research on agency response to child maltreatment, such as latent class analyses (LCA) for use as a strategy to find hidden or unknown groupings within your data (99).[19] An accessible introduction to LCA and other latent variable models can be found in Bartholomew, Steele, Moustakr and Galbraith (100) and an example of LCA using child welfare data in Abner (101).

In this chapter, we introduce topics predominantly based on a GLM approach. Starting off with a note on levels of measurement in research on agency response to child maltreatment and a reminder on weights and complex samples, the chapter focuses on the hierarchical nature of these data. We then touch on models including time and end up with a section on different software and software compatibility with statistical modelling. There are further important statistical advances for child protection research not included in this chapter, such as propensity score matching, which is an approach for improving programme evaluation (102). Other methods and techniques are available from the resources listed below.

4.1 Agency response and levels of measurement

Note that most questions associated with analyses of decision-making – whether in CPS or elsewhere – are binary coded (report yes/no, referral yes/no, service yes/no) or categorical (what type of services is provided). Linear modelling is therefore often inappropriate, and researchers can make better use of models in the log-link family. Many textbooks on statistics focus on linear models and only refer to logistic models as an expansion. However, there are a few exceptions; recommended readings are listed below.

---

[19] LCA is often characterized as a categorical data analogue to factor analysis (103).

Apart from binary or categorical outcome data, counts of events are prevalent in research on child protection services provision – the number of service referrals, the number of recurrent reports, etc. The distribution of counts is often 'L-curved', with 0 rather than 1 most prevalent and only rare occurrences of high counts. Assumptions of models based on a normal distribution do not apply; an alternative probability distribution is labelled Poisson distribution.[20] However, most models for normally distributed data are also transferable to Poisson-distributed data (and other probability distributions). The syntax structure remains the same; only the command differs (e.g. in Stata, the syntax of linear multilevel models starting with the command xtreg transfers to logistic and Poisson models and their command xtlogit or xtpoisson).

4.1.1 Further readings

▶ Hilbe J. Logistic regression models. Boca Raton: CRC Press; 2009.

▶ Hosmer DW, Lemeshow S. Applied Logistic Regression. 3rd ed. New York: John Wiley & Sons; 2013.

4.2 Using weights in complex samples

A statistical challenge in analysing surveys is the application of weights. As it is essential to conceptualize weights right from the start to collect the necessary information for calculating them, we have already introduced different weights and caveats associated with weighting your cases above (see **BOX 1.5** in **SECTION 1.3**). Although the calculation of many statistics is based on the assumption that the data were collected through a simple random sample, this is almost never the case for survey data. They are based on what are termed complex samples involving stratification and other techniques. As most surveys do not utilize simple random samples, corrections of the calculation of the statistics – by using weights – are needed. Caution should be used when computing inferential statistics with weighted data (104): Weighting can artificially reduce the variance in certain types of variables and may result in an underestimate of the standard error and inflated significance tests. To handle weights correctly for variance estimates, specialized software such as SUDAAN[21] or WesVar[22] (cf. **SECTION 4.5**) might be needed (104–106). Due to the complexity, correctly creating and using weights in surveys based on complex samples is best addressed with the support of a statistician.

4.2.1 Further readings

▶ Valliant R, Dever JA, Kreuter F). Practical tools for designing and weighting survey samples. New York: Springer; 2013.

These tools address issues in weighting survey samples for a statistically advanced audience in the social sciences.

4.3 Multilevel modelling

When analysing agency response to child maltreatment, researchers are confronted with data that are collected at different levels: child, family, child protection worker, agency and jurisdiction (e.g. county, district, province). The different levels commonly have a hierarchical structure, as children are nested in families, families are served by the respective local CPS,

---

[20] For an 'excessive' number of individuals with a count of 0 many statistical software packages also provide users with zero-inflated Poisson models.

[21] For details on SUDAAN software, see http://www.rti.org/sudaan/.

[22] For details on WesVar, see http://www.westat.com/our-work/information-systems/wesvar%C2%AE-support.

and so on (the individual child would be the level-one unit, family the level-two and agency the level-three unit). Multilevel models are a powerful tool to analyse nested structures, because they take into account correlations between subjects within the same group as distinct from correlations between groups (107). Moreover, ignoring hierarchies in data violates the assumption of independence of factors in regression analyses and will result in models that have the wrong standard errors on group-affected coefficients.

Multilevel models are an extension to conventional regression frameworks (108). Note, however, that they can also be fitted via structural equation modelling (109, 110). Different texts will introduce you to the equations and basic concepts in detail (see **SECTION 4.2.1**). This section will only briefly touch on terms and concepts that you will encounter and need to be familiar with:

▶ **Fixed and random coefficients:** Multilevel models calculate a regression line per group, for example per agency. If we assume the x-axis to be severity of maltreatment and the y-axis the victims' depressivity, we might hypothesize that the mean depressivity and therefore the intercept of the regression line will vary for different agencies. However, the direction and strength of association between severity of maltreatment and depressivity – or the regression line's slope – should be the same across agencies. This basic model is labelled random intercept-fixed slope (107). If depressivity is replaced by clients' satisfaction with services, we might assume not only different intercepts per agency but also the varying slopes that compose a random intercepts-random slopes model (**FIG. 4.1**).

Fig. 4.1 Graphical comparison of models with random intercepts and fixed or random slopes

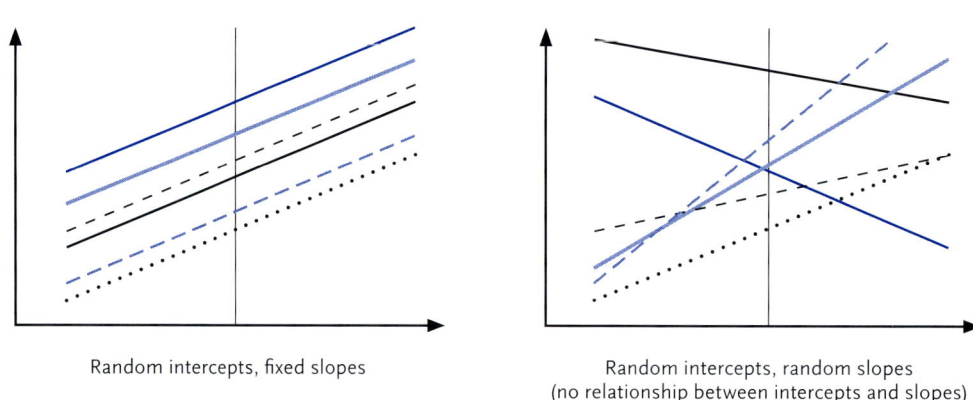

Random intercepts, fixed slopes

Random intercepts, random slopes
(no relationship between intercepts and slopes)

▶ **Assumptions:** Overall, multilevel models share assumptions with other major general linear models. However, the assumption of independence of observations is not required, as multilevel models by design assume that data from the same context are more similar than data from different contexts (111).

▶ Indices of goodness of fit reveal how well your data, or part of the data, correspond to your model. The residuals are an important expression of this. Adding a nested layer to your model should improve model fit. Generally, multilevel models are fitted by comparing different stages of model development; a constant only model (null or empty model) is set as a benchmark, comparing it to a model with first level covariates only and then adding the nested layers.

▶ When adding nested layers to your model, measures of heterogeneity between groups are needed. For logistic models, the median odds ratio translates the variance between, for example, agencies into the widely used and intuitively interpretable odds ratio scale (112). If your model is based on a linear regression, intraclass correlation will serve the same function.

An important consideration in applying multilevel models is that they can serve more than one methodological purpose. First and foremost these techniques control for the effect of shared variance within groups (clusters). Typically, this affects the error of the parameter estimates of statistical models, and if uncontrolled, it increases the chances of committing a Type I (false positive) error. The second, and methodologically more interesting purpose is being able to formulate and test hypotheses about higher level features on the dependent variables.

4.3.1 Further readings

Introductions to multilevel modelling

There are various textbooks to introduce you to multilevel modelling. However, many focus on a specific statistical software package, and some may be written at too technical a level for many social scientists, creating barriers to using these techniques that are essential for their inherently hierarchical data. The following recommended readings are written for researchers in applied social sciences and are enriched with examples.

▶ Bickel R. Multilevel analysis for applied research: it's just regression!. New York: The Guilford Press; 2007.

▶ Snijders TAB, Bosker RJ. Multilevel Analysis: An introduction to basic and advanced multilevel modelling. 2nd ed. London: Sage; 2011.

Illustrative articles using multilevel modelling in the context of child maltreatment incidence

▶ Almeida J, Cohen AP, Subramanian SV, Molnar BE. Are increased worker caseloads in state child protective service agencies a potential explanation for the decline in child sexual abuse? A multilevel analysis. Child Abuse Negl. 2008; 32(3): 367–375.

▶ Bai Y, Wells R, Hillemeier MM. Coordination between child welfare agencies and mental health service providers, children's service use, and outcomes. Child Abuse Negl. 2009; 33(6): 372–381.

▶ Fluke JD, Chabot M, Fallon B, MacLaurin B, Blackstock C. Placement decisions and disparities among Aboriginal groups: An application of the decision making ecology through multi-level analysis. Child Abuse Negl. 2010; 34(1): 57–69.

▶ Jud A, Fallon B, Trocmé N. Who gets services and who does not? Multi-level approach to the decision for ongoing child welfare or referral to specialized services. Child Youth Serv Rev. 2012; 34(5): 983–988.

▶ Walsh K, Bridgstock R, Farrell A, Rassafiani M, Schweitzer R. Case, teacher and school characteristics influencing teachers' detection and reporting of child physical abuse and neglect: Results from an Australian survey. Child Abuse Negl. 2008; 32(10): 983–993.

4.4   Analyses including 'time'

Agency response to child maltreatment is structured by different decision points (74). The continuum starts at intake and covers the decisions to investigate, provide services or remove the child, and ends at case closure. If you decide to include longitudinal data, the events in time can be conceptualized in two ways (113): First, we can observe the situations subjects are in at particular points in the time period (for example, we might record the child's well-being at intake, at referral to a service and at follow-up three months later). Second, we can monitor transitions between situations (for example, moving from being placed out of home to reunification with the family). Finally, researchers in the field are likely to be interested in recording duration (how long a child has been placed in a specific care facility, for example).

A first category of statistical models to analyse longitudinal data are time series analyses. They usually refer to a long sequence of aggregate data – about 50 data points is considered a minimum (113). Given the lack of long-term disaggregate surveillance of agency response to child maltreatment, the options for applying time series in the context of this toolkit is limited. Yet, for some countries or regions, quarterly or monthly extractions of aggregate data on service provision are available, and time series analyses are therefore an option (114).[23] Analyses of longitudinal data are not restricted to long sequences of data points. They are also possible when comparing the results of repeated cross-sectional surveys, e.g. the findings of the Netherlands' NPM-2005 and NPM-2010 cycles (117). Including time in repeated cross-sectional surveys is generally quite straightforward, by introducing time periods as a set of dummy variables with the first time period as the reference category (113). Unlike repeated cross-sectional surveys, panel and cohort studies assess changes in individuals. Panels have to deal with the quite practical problems of large costs and attrition, and they also have to account for a particular problem that has become known as panel conditioning (113): participation in a panel and knowledge of the purpose of the research may lead to responses in one wave being influenced by responses from previous waves. The multilevel models introduced above are an elegant way to include time in panel analysis: the level-one units are measurement occasions, and the level-two units are individual subjects (agencies might still be introduced as a third-level unit). Often, change between measurement occasions follows a curvilinear pattern rather than a linear pattern. Researchers will have to adapt the syntax to model the trend of the growth curve (e.g. by using a polynomial to approximate the function (108)).

Probably even more important for surveys on agency response to child maltreatment is the analysis of transition from one key event to another and the length of time until that transition. This has been quite extensively studied for out-of-home placement, by comparing children placed in foster care to children not placed at the time of comparison, the length of time to first placement, the length of time between first and subsequent placement, the length of time until reunification, etc. (115–117). This second category of analyses including time is labelled event history modelling and is traditionally often referred to as survival modelling and may be better known by this name. These techniques were originally developed by demographers to understand how time influences the likelihood of mortality and comorbidity. Although the nomenclature might appear odd or even offensive, there is an implicit interest in processes of 'survival' in research on agency response in child protection: how long does the effect of a CPS intervention last (or 'survive') until it fails (and the child is re-reported)? Or, similarly, how does the number of previous placements affect the duration of an ongoing placement? Whereas units in an event history data set are at any given point in time "at risk" of experiencing

[23] Time series analysis is a technical and specialized branch of statistics (113); applications of and introductions to time series analysis are most commonly found in the context of macroeconomics (118).

the transition from one situation to another, some units are not observed experiencing the particular event (e.g. report, referral, service provision) during the period of observation. These units are known as 'right censored'. On the other hand, 'left-truncation' occurs if the history of units in a data set is unobserved prior to the first date of data collection. Almost all data sets in agency response to child maltreatment will be truncated, as some children might have been referred to CPS previously. The general concept of event history models is readily understandable for nonadvanced researchers in statistics, but a tricky component of event history models is the need to account for covariates having values that change over time, that is, time-varying covariates (119). Note that event history data may be modelled with a wide variety of statistical models, multilevel models among them. For this purpose the data are transformed to the person-period format, which is a two-level format with time periods nested within individuals, and with a binary outcome of the event having occurred or not yet occurred (108). Nesting the individuals within agencies or geographic units will add a third level to your hierarchical structure.

4.4.1 Further readings

Introductions to analyses with longitudinal data

▶ Box-Steffensmeier JM, Jones BS. Event history modeling: A guide for social scientists. Cambridge: University Press; 2004.

▶ Tarling R. Statistical modelling for social researchers: Principles and practice. London: Routledge; 2009.

Illustrative articles analysing longitudinal data

▶ Lipien L, Forthofer, MS. An event history analysis of recurrent child maltreatment reports in Florida. Child Abuse Negl. 2004; 28(9): 947–966.

▶ Rosenthal JA, Villegas S. Placement stability for children adjudicated as dependent: a survival analysis of a state database. J Pub Child Welfare. 2011; 5(1): 67–86.

▶ Esposito T, Trocmé N, Chabot M, Shlonsky A, Collin-Vézina D, Sinha V. Placement of children in out-of-home care in Québec, Canada: when and for whom initial out-of-home placement is most likely to occur. Child Youth Serv Rev. 2014; 35(12): 2031–2039.

▶ Friedman LS, Sheppard S, Friedman D. A retrospective cohort study of suspected child maltreatment cases resulting in hospitalization. Injury. 2012; 43(11): 1881–1887. doi:10.1016/j.injury.2012.07.192

4.5 Statistical software

Commonly, researchers use the statistical software they were introduced to in their bachelor's and master's degree courses at university, or, even more simply, the software that is available to them. This is usually SPSS or, increasingly, Stata. The author agrees with Tarling (113) that "although SPSS is easy to use and has many strengths, it is somewhat frustrating for statistical modelling [...] each component is different in the terminology it adopts, its facilities for handling categorical data, creating interaction terms and other ways". Further, SPSS does not support all of the more advanced techniques described above, or only if you purchase the additional package SPSS Advanced Statistics. Stata may be a little more difficult to learn initially, but it does have a unifying framework with commands following a consistent pattern (113). The software fits a wider range of models and also benefits from a large user base, members of which create additional routines that are available and can be incorporated within Stata (113). The advantages and disadvantages of other all-in-one solutions such as R or SAS, Mplus and model-specific software for multilevel modelling (MLwiN, HLM, etc.) and SEM (Amos, LISREL, Latent Gold, etc.) are detailed by Tarling (113).

4.5.1 Further resources

An accessible and easy-to-read online summary of survey analysis software is provided by Zaslavsky at http://www.hcp.med.harvard.edu/statistics/survey-soft/. The summary focuses on the analyses of surveys with complex samples and software that can do variance estimation with such survey data. However, it has not been updated recently and the latest developments in all-in-one software solutions are not incorporated.

5. Collaboration between research and practice

5.1 Obtaining agency participation

Successfully obtaining the participation of agencies and frontline professionals is not only essential for representative research on agency response to child maltreatment, but also essential to its reliability. The more frontline professionals perceive research as relevant, the more they are motivated to participate and the more they will adhere to manuals and definitions for data collection, gather data more accurately, and produce fewer missing responses. In this chapter, strategies to obtain successful participation are presented within a framework of knowledge mobilization. Readers are then familiarized with some obstacles to participation and strategies to overcome them. The examples in this chapter are drawn from previous surveys on child maltreatment incidence.

5.1.1 *The framework of knowledge mobilization*

In collecting data, researchers usually focus on trying to generalize knowledge beyond local instances, whereas policy-makers and institutional service providers tend to put more value on local knowledge and specific circumstances (*120, 121*). The different cultures surrounding people doing research and people who might be able to use and apply their findings sometimes leads to finger-pointing (*122*): "Decision-makers accuse researchers of irrelevant, poorly communicated 'products'; researchers accuse decision-makers of political expediency that results in irrational outcomes." Efforts are therefore needed to translate methods and findings to decision-makers and to familiarize researchers with local knowledge and issues of concern in current practice (*121, 123*). The stakeholders in policy and practice will commit to participation only if the research initiative is perceived as being both relevant to the stakeholders and credible. Relevance and credibility, in turn, can only be reached through a trusted partnership between researchers and decision-makers (*122*).

A commitment of agencies in child protection (or other applied areas) to participate has to be accompanied by a collaborative effort in planning, producing and disseminating research. This emerging collaborative approach between researchers and stakeholders in policy and practice has been labelled knowledge translation or knowledge mobilization (*120, 124*).[24] The term knowledge mobilization "embodies the idea that the use of knowledge is a social process, not just an intellectual task, and as such, multidirectional. At the same time, 'mobilization' implies effort and direction, not just random interaction" (*120*). In this chapter, the term 'knowledge mobilization' is used as a more general term to address the research-practice gap, whereas knowledge translation will be referred to as a process within the broader frame of knowledge mobilization. It involves the process of making research interpretable to stakeholders in practice and making the diversity and complexities of local contexts accessible to researchers.
....

[24] Further terms such as knowledge exchange or knowledge transfer are used to describe this emerging approach to share data (*120, 124*).

In the field of health services, there is a considerable body of research on the common elements that make the collaborative effort of knowledge mobilization successful both in terms of: (1) the production of relevant and timely information through well-integrated partnerships between researchers, policy-makers and service providers; and (2) the development of capacity within policy-making and service provider organizations to integrate research information and build up a culture of trust and credibility (121). The following points summarize Trocmé et al.'s (121) more detailed overview:

▶ **Knowledge production partnerships** between researchers and practitioners are reciprocal in nature. For the collaborative effort to succeed, the investment of time and other resources has to be identified as worthwhile by both parties. Whereas practitioners might be eager to have valid arguments for obtaining resources for their services from policy-makers, researchers need the prospect of disseminating their findings in the academic world.

▶ **Building trust between researchers and decision-makers** is key for arriving at a knowledge production partnership. Trust is developed and nurtured through positive experiences and consistent contact, both formal and informal (face-to-face meetings, regular emails and telephone calls, etc.).

▶ **Relevance and timeliness:** To start a research project on the agency response to child maltreatment, researchers need to ensure that the topic is perceived as relevant by stakeholders (or in some cases, to convince stakeholders of a survey's relevance). In our experience, practitioners quite readily accepted the benefit of potentially identifying under- and overreporting for certain regions, gaps in service provision, etc. A higher barrier to the implementation of the knowledge mobilization approach to research is timeliness. The research timeline often does not allow for researchers to have findings available as quickly as desired by practitioners.

▶ **The importance of context-specific knowledge:** Whereas researchers look out for generalizable knowledge, agencies and frontline workers are concerned that material appearing in international journals may not apply to their context. Workers participating in the CIS, for example, often felt that the study's findings would have relevance at the macro level but not for their work on the frontline (15). Efforts by researchers to understand and appreciate the need for context-specific knowledge will not only improve the commitment of sampled agencies, but also help to identify factors facilitating or hindering the transfer of findings into practice.

▶ **Supporting knowledge utilization:** Professionals who are comfortable with research terminology and perceive themselves as capable of critically appraising research articles will more readily embrace a research initiative on agency response to child maltreatment. Building capacity to use empirical findings and an organizational culture and management that value them are important factors to encourage knowledge utilization.[25]

Although framing your research in a knowledge mobilization approach is likely to improve agency participation, it brings with it challenges in communicating with authorities in the academic world. Feldman (125) pointed out "the strong bias of the review committees toward methodological purity, even to the detriment of utility." In the following sections we will present successful strategies used in previous agency surveys on the incidence of child maltreatment. Even though not necessarily developed in a knowledge mobilization framework, they generally value the participating agency as a partner in producing knowledge.

---

[25] Researchers can contribute to knowledge utilization by making practice-relevant information readily available. An example can be found at http://www.ican4kids.org/.

Dissemination as an essential part of this concept will be addressed in a separate section (see **SECTION 5.3**). Overall, we strongly recommend building in plenty of time for buy-in, recruitment, approval of administrators, and access to frontline staff (e.g. social workers in a public child protection service or paediatricians in a hospital child protection team), as participation is key to representativeness and will maximize the impact of your research on agency response to child maltreatment. Based on their experience with three CIS-cycles, Fallon et al. (*15*) identified the following phases and timelines: (I) contracting: 12 months, (II) planning: 12 months, (III) data collection: 12 months, and (IV) data cleaning and reporting: 18 months.

5.1.2 Preparatory work

The road to the successful participation of agencies and frontline staff starts even before recruitment through anticipating and identifying issues that are core to practitioners and might be addressed by your research on mapping agency response to child maltreatment. Issues are identified through meeting with professionals at regional conferences, through continuing education for decision-makers, or through students in practical training at agencies.

The many disciplines in the child protection system use different terms and codes. Stakeholders are easily disconnected if they think researchers are not familiar enough with their fields and their specific contexts. If your survey is to include professionals from different backgrounds, a preparatory strategy might be to develop a glossary of terms for the related disciplines and regions, along with an understanding of issues that the stakeholders are currently grappling with. This includes monitoring changes in the legislative and structural context that may present barriers or opportunities for data collection (e.g. implementation of differential response versus the investigative track in various states of the United States (*126*)).

Research terminology can often be confusing or off-putting to practitioners, so a glossary will also help improve the accessibility of your project title, invitation letters, executive summary, etc. Instead of framing your project as, for example, an 'incidence study', investigators of previous agency surveys have suggested alternatives, such as studies on "child reporting and disposition", "professional needs assessment for your area", "mapping the needs of children to increase and maintain integrity of the family", etc. You might also want to put in a good deal of effort to explain how agencies could use the data to develop more and better services or explain that the findings might influence the setting of national policies, the allocation of resources to prevention programmes, etc. However, keep in mind that you should clarify questions that the data can and cannot answer (*127*).

In addition to terms, codes and customs also vary between disciplines. Therefore, you might want to explore different procedures for initiating the first contact.[26] Professionals at court probably prefer a more formal style, letters instead of emails. Whereas invitation letters for sampled agencies are a mandatory step, other means of communication may better set the groundwork for obtaining agency participation, such as releasing media or policy briefs (for the use of media releases and policy briefs in disseminating findings, see **CHAPTER 5.3**).

5.1.3 Finding collaborators

Collaborating with the right people was a major key to the success of previous agency studies. The process has to include people serving in different functions – agency administrators,

---

[26] Preparatory tasks will include not only exploring different procedures in initiating contact but also figuring out who the key administrator or first contact in the agency is (see the following section for more details).

frontline staff, co-investigators, and other researchers, community members, government officials, and agency staff whose buy-in will be key to completing the study successfully. Strategies to enhance participation through endorsements of different groups are outlined below.

One approach that can increase context-specific knowledge is to conduct research using a multisite team. In multilingual countries such as Belgium, Canada or Switzerland, members of the minority linguistic group can feel marginalized by the majority group[27] *(128)*. Agencies and frontline workers' acceptance of a survey is likely to improve if the research team has branches in all major regions. In Canada, the team of the CIS was located not only at two sites in the Anglophone parts of the country, but also in Francophone Québec *(129)*. A multisite team might be beneficial not only for multilingual countries, but also for nations with historical difficulties or economic and/or cultural differences between regions. For example, a multisite team might be helpful in Italy, with a location in both the northern and southern regions, or in the United Kingdom with locations in England, Northern Ireland, Scotland and Wales.

To facilitate participation, political buy-in and influential allies are needed. Preferably, some of the facilitators are political and societal authorities. Facilitators are not necessarily restricted to a regional or national level; support from international bodies, such as UNICEF or WHO, might be helpful for buy-in by agencies in several countries. **BOX 5.1** on obtaining stakeholder commitment for data collection in Saudi Arabia reveals the importance of involving not only political allies and different disciplines working with children, but also the public.

At least as important is obtaining acceptance and commitment from the agency professionals who you will be working with. It might help to get assistance from regionally or even nationally well-known experts who embrace the study and its aims; and particularly, if they are available, professionals with a dual role of practitioner and researcher/academic. If different disciplines are involved – such as social work, psychology, medicine – each of them must be addressed separately. You may also want to get approval from a national umbrella organization in the child protection sector (social work or psychological association, etc.). Consultation with these individuals and groups will help you to understand and anticipate the impact of political fault lines and better describe how the study can respond to a range of competing interests. An interdisciplinary study team can also be a valuable strategy for gaining buy-in from different disciplines. Further, in several nations it may be important to focus particular attention to collaboration issues when collecting data on agency responses to maltreated children from Aboriginal populations or other ethnic minorities. Historically, Aboriginal peoples have often been oppressed and denied basic human rights. It might therefore be helpful to treat data collection associated with Aboriginal populations with extra care. The CIS, for example, "has a strong commitment to honouring the principles of Aboriginal Ownership of, Control over, Access to, and Possession of research conducted in Aboriginal contexts (OCAP principles)" *(36)*.

Another important component of preparatory work is securing the commitment of key administrators. To facilitate efficient and successful data collection, key administrators should be involved at an early stage to discuss the procedure of obtaining access to staff and files. Once a key administrator is identified, a strategy for buy-in is to broach the topic with a close mutual contact (if available) before formally issuing the invitation. The processes of obtaining formal approval may vary, based on legal frame and organizational culture; if child protection is county- or even municipality-administered, the local director of the child protection agency will be responsible for approval of participation. In places where child protection is subject

---

[27] The feeling might be fed by historical experiences *(130)*, even if a current research initiative has no tendency to culturally dominate parts of a country.

to top-down organization, at the provincial level or even centrally for the whole nation (25), approval is sometimes needed from upper-level administrators who may be quite removed from the day-to-day protection work. While the approval of an executive director will assure participation of all the agency's branches, a risk associated with higher-level administration is that the agreement might not trickle down to frontline workers (15). Those more directly involved with frontline work, although holding less relative power, may be the key to obtaining local agency participation. In county- or municipality-administered child protection, it might be more crucial to ally with practice-experienced champions in child protection to commit a province's agencies to participate that have to be addressed individually. In federally organized countries, services may be administered both at the provincial, county or municipal level and different strategies are needed to guarantee administrative support at any of these levels (4).

Finally, the framework of knowledge mobilization should also be applied to frontline staff. They need to value your goals for collecting data on child maltreatment for it to be successful. Workers who are motivated to participate will collect data more reliably and produce fewer missing values compared to mandated but noncommitted participants. Trust may be built through involving a sample of frontline workers at an early stage. Other frontline staff will more readily accept the questionnaire as practice-validated, if their coworkers have had a part in its development. But training is essential for standardized data collection. Continuous assistance through hotlines, an online set of frequently asked questions, or repeated visits to the agency will ease the process of data collection for frontline staff (15). Further examples of applying these strategies are found in **BOXES 5.1 AND 5.2**.

5.1.4 *Threats to participation and incentives*

Participating in an agency survey on the incidence of child maltreatment is usually associated with several concerns by potential participants that could develop into threats to the study's success, and therefore need to be adequately addressed. For most of the issues raised, a collaborative approach of including practitioners in the development of the study and its questionnaire will be a helpful strategy to diminish the concerns.

▶ Confidentiality is a quintessential part of the interaction between professional and client and is often legally protected. Sharing details of this trusted relationship with someone else quite naturally raises concerns. Avoiding client identifiers in a survey or filtering them out in a file analysis is in accordance with research ethical guidelines and required by ethics committees, but researchers still must proactively and transparently communicate their methods of securing confidentiality to the participating agencies. Arguably, confidentiality concerns need to be treated with extra care for minority or marginalized groups. Researchers who have conducted previous agency surveys recommend planning time for meetings to address these concerns. Less-than-perfect matches to identify duplicate anonymized entries of the same case by different agencies were described elsewhere (see **SECTION 2.4**).

▶ For frontline workers and agencies, participating in a national survey on service provision is quite readily associated with concerns about being evaluated and compared. Workers might, even without reason, fear that the findings might be potentially embarrassing and might generate reprimands from superiors. In addition, making comparisons across regions might potentially be stigmatizing for certain communities and lead to discriminatory behaviours against them (e.g. finding a higher incidence of sexual abuse in a minority group). It is therefore essential to reassure participants that ranking individuals and agencies is not their interest and that potential comparisons of regions will not be used to the detriment of child protection practice. It may be necessary to formally

BOX 5.1

Obtaining stakeholder commitment in Saudi Arabia

Public discussion on child maltreatment was considered taboo in Saudi Arabian society until recently. The issue was first brought up in the 1990s, when a few case reports were published in the local health care literature (28). At this point, the public and stakeholders were thought to be ready to accept the concept of child maltreatment as a public health issue. A top-down approach, starting with buy-in from government leadership through the direct involvement of politically influential individuals, was found to be essential, along with an all-inclusive and multidisciplinary involvement of practitioners. The National Family Safety Program (NFSP) was established by royal decree and mandated with the task of prevention of child maltreatment and domestic violence (28). It was decided that the NFSP would be administratively linked to a government healthcare institution to bring forth the health and medical impact of maltreatment, a socially more acceptable means of discussing such stigmatizing behaviours. This then led to national spread of child protection teams and a national registry for reported cases of child maltreatment seeking healthcare. Although there is an underestimate of the actual prevalence of maltreatment, the registry has been seen as a major milestone in the country, as it provides some evidence to the extent of at least relatively severe cases of child maltreatment.

Stakeholder commitment was further addressed by fully engaging all stakeholders in the cause – in 'their' cause. Representation from the various stakeholders in the government was ensured in all major events and plans, including the composition of the executive board of the NFSP. The theme and slogan for each of the NFSP annual meetings were selected so as to be relevant to a different stakeholder each year. Training programmes and capacity building were developed so as to train multidisciplinary professionals, including healthcare, mental health, social services, law enforcement, and judicial professionals, and members of the clergy. The commitment of the different organizations was evidenced by various collaborative agreements with the NFSP. The public was involved through the media and community awareness programmes at public venues, schools and exhibits. Religious leaders and scholars were engaged and supported spreading the awareness in the community. Students studying overseas were reached out to through government channels to further support increasing awareness among members of society.

Research to provide the necessary evidence base for decision-making and programme and resource prioritization was given precedence. National community-based epidemiological studies were conducted as a baseline for future surveillance studies and systems. Further, a national research consortium was established and consortium membership invitations extended to all stakeholders in the government, universities and research centres. The objectives of the consortium were set to include: (1) identifying research priorities, (2) ensuring trust and credibility among researchers and institutions, (3) facilitating communication and overcoming conflicts of interest, (4) protecting participants' rights, and (5) facilitating funding and conducting timely research.

guarantee nonidentification of certain entities in publications (for example, by labelling certain Canadian provinces Eastern Region A and Eastern Region B (73)). However, this should not lead to denying participants the opportunity to eventually make comparisons that are important or may be of interest.[28]

▶ **Work burden** is potentially the biggest threat to participation. Agencies and staff in child protection are continuously struggling to allocate scarce resources to the most urgent problems (131). Many child protection workers will feel they are overworked (15). Their

---

[28] In fact, for the CIS, the most common request from the field of practice has been to compare a geographic area of interest to another region or the rest of Canada (127).

BOX 5.2

Obtaining stakeholder commitment in the BECAN project (Balkan region)

The Balkan Epidemiological Study of Child Abuse and Neglect (BECAN project, 2009–2012)[a] was co-funded by the European Union and initiated by a partnership of research institutes, universities and nongovernmental organizations in nine countries – Albania, Bosnia and Herzegovina, Bulgaria, Croatia, Greece, Romania, Serbia, the former Yugoslav Republic of Macedonia and Turkey. Along with a population survey, a case-based surveillance study (CBSS) was undertaken, aimed at identifying child maltreatment incidence rates via extracting existing data from recorded cases in archives of agencies in the field of child protection (e.g. public child protection services, health sector, police forces, nongovernmental organizations).

The preparatory phase of the CBSS included the mapping of agencies in the different countries' child protection systems. Approaching organizations to obtain participation was attempted by the research consortium via contacting either political authorities (such as relevant ministries) or individual organizations in countries where a well-structured (public) child protection system did not exist at the time. Formal and informal communication was used, including individualized invitations, informational material, meetings with agencies' or authorities' representatives, and networking activities involving frontline professionals. Considering the methodological problems associated with definitions of child maltreatment and anticipating difficulties related to the involvement of different professional groups, two strategies were applied in data collection efforts. First, eligible cases were selected by the local interdisciplinary research team on the basis of a detailed operations manual available in the official languages of the nine countries. Second, trained members of the team then extracted disaggregated data from agencies' archives in all countries. This not only increased reliability of data extraction, but also reduced workload for frontline staff (20).

Whereas in countries with a top-down approach all sampled agencies participated, the procedure was less successful in countries where no surveillance mechanisms in the context of child protection services existed. In those countries, a total of 224 invited agencies did not participate in the CBSS. A main barrier for obtaining participation (observed mainly in Greece) was a nationwide policy change: social services moved from municipalities to prefectures and it was not feasible to locate paper files for 2010 for several agencies, and no solution was found for obtaining participation from these agencies. Complaints about lack of time, confidentiality issues (in spite of procedures to anonymize cases) and concerns about being evaluated (e.g. on how they kept their records) were additional barriers to participation. In specific cases, ethical issues related to confidentiality proved to be an insurmountable obstacle for obtaining participation. In Turkey, for example, the justice system provided full access to its files and the health system partial access, but no social services or education-related services participated due to confidentiality issues. Lastly, an additional obstacle was related to the difficulty of finding and/ or maintaining contact with the agencies due to restricted channels of communication. In Greece, for example, many agencies do not use emails and contact via telephone is not always easy.

On the other hand, the national network meetings proved to be an effective incentive for committing professionals to participate. Transparency – all the material (forms and manual) was made available to agencies from the first point of contact – was another asset. The benefit of allowing agencies to use all materials for their own purposes and acknowledging an agency's participation in the study report were further incentives to participation.

....

[a] For more details, see http://www.becan.eu/node/33.

workload often exceeds what is considered manageable[29] (*132*). Extra work for data collection will conflict with work time for clients or with the worker's free time. Besides the worker's perception that the study is valid and relevant, it is therefore essential to create a questionnaire that covers important issues while not being overly lengthy.[30] As an example of good practice, we refer to an Israeli agency survey (*19*), where short questionnaires with few details were developed, and the tools were user-friendly, easy, and quick to complete. Furthermore, concise, clear language and a comfortable computer interface increased participation (Rachel Szabo-Lael, personal communication, August 3, 2014).

▶ **Transparency on financial resource**s is an important piece in building a trusted partnership between researchers and practitioners. Private foundations sponsored by companies might invest in child protection research not only out of purely altruistic motives, but also partly for a positive image. Noninterference in analyses and dissemination of important findings must be guaranteed by the foundation and proactively communicated to participants.

Apart from threats to participation, previous agency surveys have also identified incentives that improve commitment for data sharing. For agencies, the findings might be used as an opportunity to develop their documentation (including new variables in their documentation, change from paper-pencil files to fully electronic files, etc.) or develop information systems (improving processes, etc.). However, if not properly introduced, a major change in documentation or processes might be perceived as a threat in an overburdened work environment. Direct incentives, such as payment for each case entry, have also been used. However, in the first agency survey of the Optimus Study Switzerland, payment did not affect participation as much as had been hoped for (*56*). Apart from other factors limiting participation in that particular study, financial incentives did not decrease the most important barrier: work burden. Therefore, instead of investing funds in financial incentives, the resources might be better invested in keeping data collection work for agencies at a minimum, e.g. by extracting already electronically documented uniform data elements from the agency's file system or having research assistants on the premises. Finally, small tokens such as pens might not work as incentives, but they still express gratitude for participation.

Further resources

Bronfenbrenner Center for Translational Research (BCTR) http://www.bctr.cornell.edu/
"The mission of the Bronfenbrenner Center for Translational Research is to expand, strengthen, and speed the connections between cutting-edge research and the design, evaluation, and implementation of policies and practices that enhance human development, health, and well-being" (http://www.bctr.cornell.edu/about-us/mission-history/). Of special interest to researchers in the field of child protection, the BCTR is also home to the National Data Archive on Child Abuse and Neglect (http://ndacan.cornell.edu).

5.2   Cost issues in studying the national prevalence of child maltreatment: an example of a cost-effective study strategy in the Netherlands

Regularly assessing the prevalence of child abuse and neglect can yield great insights into changes in prevalence and risk factors over time. In this respect, comparing changes in prevalence rates and risk factors between countries has additional value, because it enables evaluation of the effect of (parallel) policy changes. Indeed, a recent National Research Council report lists investigating trends in the incidence of child maltreatment as one of the

---

[29] The Council on Accreditation (COA), an international independent accrediting body for public and private social services agencies, suggests that a manageable workload should not exceed 15 to 30 open cases (*133*).

[30] For an approach to a minimum data set in child maltreatment surveillance, see http://www.can-via-mds.eu.

recommended research priorities (*134*). The fact that nationwide agency-based studies are being conducted on a regular basis in very large (United States: (*9, 10*)) and small (Netherlands (*16, 17, 68*)) countries is promising with respect to their implementation in other countries.

In the most recent nationwide prevalence study of maltreatment of youth in the Netherlands, the NPM-2010 (*17, 68*), a sentinel/agency-based study was combined with a self-report study in a sample of high school students. Before planning a study of this kind, costs need to be estimated for the following main aspects: requesting permission from an ethical review board, selecting participating organizations and participants, contacting organizations and participants for permission (email and telephone), sending study materials to sentinels, aggregating and processing CPS data (including unduplication; see **CHAPTER 2**), coding sentinel case reports (including training coders), visiting high schools for the self-report study, data entry, data analysis, and writing. In addition, optional costs can be considered for creating a house style and study logo and for layout and dissemination of the report.

To achieve a national estimate of one-year prevalence[31] it is essential to select nationally representative groups of sentinels. In the Netherlands, with a relatively dense population of 16 615 400 including 3 514 478 children at the time of the study (2010), 1127 sentinels were selected from 461 organizations. Three additional samples were selected for each sentinel group in case of refusal to participate. Sentinels were selected from 12 different types of organizations: primary schools, secondary schools, shelters for battered women, well-baby clinics, home-based child care, centre-based child care, kindergartens, police forces, child protection boards, general practitioners, emergency departments, and child protection professionals in hospitals (see (*17*) for the numbers of participating organizations per organization type). To randomly select a representative set of organizations, the country was divided into five zones, each including about the same number of children. In addition, data from all Advice and Reporting Centers for Abuse (public CPS) in the Netherlands were included. All boards of organizations were contacted first to get permission to conduct the study. Next, if applicable, locations were randomly selected, and finally, professionals were randomly selected. On all of these levels, letters were sent and telephone calls made.

Similar to the NIS (*10*), sentinels were asked to fill out a form for each child for whom they suspected child abuse or neglect during a period of three months. Sentinels received instructions, including definitions of the various types of child maltreatment, by mail. In the previous Dutch prevalence study (*16, 135*) about two thirds of the participating sentinels were trained in person to use the research materials. However, results indicated that there were no differences in the number of cases reported by sentinels who attended and did not attend the instruction meeting (*16*). So, in the second NPM, instruction materials were mailed to the sentinels. At the end of the study, all participating sentinels were contacted by telephone to ask if they had indeed participated, even when they had not reported a child for whom maltreatment was suspected.

The sentinels sent back 818 forms in total. After removing cases that did not meet the inclusion criteria (e.g. maltreatment took place outside the research period, victims were 18 years or older), did not meet the definitions of child maltreatment, or were duplicates, 760 cases were used in the analyses. All case descriptions were coded by reliable coders to assign maltreatment status and types of maltreatment. **TABLE 5.1** lists the numbers of organizations, participants, and cases in the NPM-2010.

For universities, the costs can be relatively limited, because trained undergraduate and graduate students can be involved in different steps of the study in the context of their training

....

[31] The number of cases in one year, irrespective of whether they are first-time cases or not.

or dissertation research. The NPM-2010 was conducted by a university in collaboration with a research institute, with the majority of research assistants being undergraduate and graduate students. In total, the research team consisted of five senior researchers (part-time) and 13 students and other research assistants (full- and part-time). The study commenced in spring 2010, and the final report was delivered in summer 2011. The NPM was funded by the Dutch Ministry of Health, Welfare and Sport (similar to the NIS, funded by the United States' Congress, and the CIS, core funded by the Public Health Agency of Canada), but other government funds, private foundations, or nongovernmental organizations may also provide (part of) the funding.

TABLE 5.1

Numbers of organizations, participants, and cases in the second Dutch prevalence study with a total population of 3 514 478 children (NPM-2010) (17, 68)

SENTINEL STUDY	NUMBER
Organizations	416 (plus three additional samples per organization type, in case of refusal to participate)
Sentinels	1 127 (plus three additional samples per organization, in case of refusal to participate)
Case descriptions sent back by sentinels	818
CPS locations	15
Cases substantiated by CPS	22 661

5.3   Dissemination

Once the study has been completed, its findings should be actively disseminated to ensure that the study reaches the intended audience and to maximize its impact. In the field of dissemination and implementation research, dissemination is defined as a formal and active approach to spreading research findings to the target audience or audiences using determined channels and a planned strategy to stimulate adoption and enhance the integration of the findings or evidence into routine practice (136, 137). Dissemination is often viewed as a first stage along a continuum followed by adoption, implementation and sustainability (136) (on sustainability, see **SECTION 5.4** below). In contrast, diffusion is defined as the passive, untargeted, unplanned and uncontrolled spread of new interventions or research findings (137).

Most dissemination models and approaches aim to achieve the following three main broad goals:

▶   increase reach to a variety of audiences using various media;

▶   increase motivation to use and apply the information, including through champions, opinion or thought leaders, or social networks;

▶   increase ability to use and apply evidence, by, for instance, providing additional resources on how it can be incorporated into current practice or specific suggestions for change (136).

As early as possible in the research process a dissemination plan should be developed that clearly addresses each of the following five key questions: (1) What is the message?, (2) What is the audience?, (3) Who is the messenger?, (4) What are the transfer methods or media to be used?, and (5) What is the expected outcome? (*138*, *139*):

1. **What is the message?** The content of the message will largely depend on the research question or questions that the mapping exercise set out to answer – whether the study primarily aims to assess the current state of development of the legal, health and social service agencies responding to child maltreatment in a country; or explore the nature of agencies responding to child maltreatment and the nature of their response; or estimate the incidence of child maltreatment in the country, etc. In all cases, however, it is important that the message be based closely on the findings of the study, expressed in actionable terms, tailored to the particular needs of the audience, and be as clear, concise and compelling as possible, as well as logical. An example of good practice in messaging is the publication Sexual victimization of children and adolescents in Switzerland (*18*).

2. **What is the audience?** It is important to define the audience and engage with them as early on as possible to understand their information needs and tailor the disseminated information to increase the likelihood of it being taken up and used. The audiences for the findings of the mapping exercise are multiple and will, again, partly depend on the exact research question that the mapping exercise is addressing. Nonetheless, potential audiences can be divided into the following broad categories: (i) persons responsible for and involved in high-level decisions concerning the development of services to respond to child maltreatment in a country; these will include, for instance, policy-makers, funders and programme commissioners belonging to governmental, nongovernmental, international, and private organizations; (ii) agencies and professional groups providing services; (iii) organizations representing service users and particularly high-risk or vulnerable populations (e.g. survivors and victim groups, children with disabilities, marginalized groups, etc.); (iv) advocates who are trying to increase the political priority of child protection and child maltreatment prevention, who may be part of the government, nongovernmental organizations, community-based organizations, the media, etc.; (v) researchers; (vi) the scientific press; and (vii) the mainstream media, as a potential means to reach the former groups and the general public. Efforts should be made to engage with them as early on as possible to inform them of the project and to explore their information needs. This can be done, for instance, through brief presentations or seminars, fact sheets describing the project, with a brief questionnaire asking about how best to tailor the dissemination to the audience's needs, or telephone conversations.

3. **Who is the messenger?** The key consideration here is for messengers to have credibility in the eyes of the audience. Ensuring that the study is either carried out or visibly sponsored by organizations in the country with credibility in the field of child protection and child maltreatment prevention – such as a government agency, a reputable research institute or university, or a large nongovernmental organizations or international organization – will lend weight to the findings. Ensuring that logos of these credible organizations are prominently displayed on products to be disseminated can be important in this regard. Employing representatives of this credible organization or high-profile champions or advocates (e.g. politicians, celebrities, high-profile scientists) to help disseminate the findings may also increase its impact.

4. **What are the transfer methods or media to be used?** This will depend on available resources and which of the audiences defined above are being targeted. The various

products through which dissemination will occur should be available on the website of the organization that conducted the research, and links to the website should be available from as many partner organizations' websites as possible. The products may include the following: the full research report; a summary of the full report; policy and research briefs; press releases; flyers, posters, factsheets, brochures and infographics; ready-made material for social media (e.g. Facebook posts, Tweets) and generic PowerPoint presentations (which can then be adapted); video and audio clips, including statements of support by prominent champions; training materials derived from the findings (i.e. PowerPoint presentations, facilitators notes, hand-outs); prerecorded webinars; scientific papers based on the research; press articles on the findings; etc. In addition, findings from the study should be presented at academic conferences and meetings of stakeholders whenever possible.

Among these different dissemination media, the following should be given priority in relation to each of these audiences outlined:

i. Persons responsible for and involved in high-level decisions concerning the development of services:

▶ policy briefs summarizing findings and relating them to current policy debates and outlining rationales for choosing a particular policy choice;

▶ flyers, posters, factsheets, brochures and infographics summarizing research findings in a concise and visually appealing way; efforts should be made to feature these on their websites;

▶ short presentations, seminars, or webinars geared towards policy-makers, parliamentarians, think tanks, and political parties, as part of regular seminar or webinar series, for instance. Recruiting a high-visibility champion to deliver these will add to their impact.

ii. Agencies and professional groups providing services:

▶ research briefs, summary of the full report, and full report – featured on agency websites or in agency newsletters, if possible;

▶ flyers, posters, factsheets, brochures and infographics;

▶ interactive workshops presenting findings and exploring implications for practitioners;

▶ presentations, seminars or webinars for agencies or professional associations; these may include individualized analyses of the data of particular interest to the agencies or professional groups;

▶ short videos presenting findings – perhaps by a well-known champion – that can be hosted on the agencies' or professional associations' websites;

▶ ready-made material for social media (e.g. Facebook posts, Tweets) and generic PowerPoint presentations (which can then be adapted);

▶ create networks or communities of practice to connect people who might not otherwise be connected to share knowledge and improve professional practice. An example of such a community of practice is the United States-based eXtension Alliance for Better Child Care Community of Practice,[32] which aims to create a

---

[32] For details, see http://www.extension.org/pages/25362/extension-alliance-for-better-child-care-community-of-practice-description#.VDJOQoocSUk

collaborative educational resource for professionals who serve child care providers, families and communities seeking early childhood information and resources, and to provide appropriate information and learning opportunities that are science-based, peer-reviewed and timely.

iii. Organizations representing service users and particularly high-risk or vulnerable populations (e.g. children with disabilities, marginalized groups, etc.)

▶ research briefs, summary of full report, and full research report – featured on organizations' websites or in their newsletters if possible;

▶ flyers, posters, factsheets, brochures, and infographics;

▶ interactive workshops presenting findings, highlighting findings particularly relevant to these groups;

▶ presentations, seminars or webinars for these organizations, which may include individualized analyses of the data of particular interest to them;

▶ short videos presenting findings – perhaps by a well-known champion – that can be hosted on these organizations' websites;

▶ ready-made material for social media (e.g. Facebook posts, Tweets) and generic PowerPoint presentations (which can then be adapted).

iv. Advocates:

▶ research and policy briefs, executive summary, and full research report;

▶ ready-made PowerPoint presentations that they can use;

▶ infographics and short videos;

▶ ready-made material for social media (e.g. Facebook posts, Tweets) and generic PowerPoint presentations (which can then be adapted).

v. Researchers:

▶ research and policy briefs, executive summary, and full research report;

▶ scientific papers;

▶ training material derived from findings;

▶ provided data are appropriately anonymized and copyright considerations are respected, making the full dataset available to researchers for further analyses should be considered.

vi. Scientific press: It is important to publish findings in national and/or international peer-reviewed scientific journals, aiming for those with the highest impact factor. Although the actual readership of scientific journals is often limited, publishing the findings in a peer-reviewed journal will boost the credibility of the findings in the eyes of policy-makers, practitioners, other researchers, and journalists.

vii. The mainstream media, as a potential means to reach the former groups and the general public:

▶ Press releases, media briefs.

▶ Press conferences.

▶ Ready-made text, pictures, video clips and footage to make covering the research results easier.

▶ Cultivate relations with print, television, radio, and web-based journalists with a view to persuading them to cover the study findings.

▶ Have spokespersons with media experience prepared to give interviews.

▶ Use high-profile champions to draw the attention of journalists.

5. **What is the expected outcome?** At least two different types of expected outcomes should be distinguished and, as much as possible, kept separate: scientific outcomes and advocacy outcomes. The expected scientific outcome should be to communicate the findings with the greatest clarity and accuracy, to ensure that the findings reach the scientists working in this area, and to contribute towards increasing scientific knowledge in the area of child protection and child maltreatment prevention. Expected advocacy outcomes will partly depend on the research findings and the extent of the gaps and weaknesses identified in child protection. If warranted, the expected advocacy outcome can be summed up as increasing the political priority of and investment in the issue to address the gaps and weaknesses and, perhaps also, ensure the regular repetition of such mapping exercises. To achieve expected advocacy outcomes, it is critical that the research report and the derived communications products contain concrete practical recommendations for action. Giving examples of success stories – from within the country or from without – of how others have managed to address the identified gaps or weaknesses and further resources – e.g. websites and references to publications – can also be useful.

Funds for a sustained dissemination strategy that includes the development of at least some of the products listed above will have to be included in the budget from the start. Sufficient time to prepare and disseminate these products will also have to be factored in. Ideally, the various communications products derived from the research findings should be ready when the main report is launched.

Further resources

The United States' Centers for Disease Control and Prevention has a very useful Gateway to communication practice and social marketing, where you can access a wealth of resources relevant to dissemination. For more information, see http://www.cdc.gov/healthcommunication/.

Communication and dissemination strategies to facilitate the use of health-related evidence (136) is a systematic research review that focuses on "promoting informed decisions about health-related behaviors and decisions among patients and clinicians. First, it addresses the comparative effectiveness of communicating evidence in various contents and formats that increase the likelihood that target audiences will both understand and use the information. Second, it examines the comparative effectiveness of a variety of approaches for disseminating evidence from those who develop it to those who are expected to use it. Third, it examines the comparative effectiveness of various ways of communicating uncertainty associated with health-related evidence to different target audiences, including evidence translators, health educators, patients, and clinicians" (136). The executive summary and the full report of the review are available at http://effectivehealthcare.ahrq.gov/index.cfm/search-for-guides-reviews-and-reports/?productid=1756&pageaction=displayproduct

From research to practice: a knowledge transfer planning guide (139) is a very useful guide that teaches the nuts and bolts of knowledge transfer by taking the user through a set of practical thinking exercises. It is available at http://www.iwh.on.ca/from-research-to-practice

5.4   Sustainability

A project is sustainable when it continues to deliver benefits to the project beneficiaries and/ or the community for an extended period after the initial funding has ceased (140). Although it may prove difficult to guarantee a project's future impacts with absolute certainty, a number of tangible actions can be taken from the very outset to increase project sustainability. Whereas financial and human capacities will unavoidably vary over time, immediate benefits as well as long-term sustainability will be bolstered by a combination of effective multi-stakeholder communication, continuous monitoring and evaluation of project activities, a strong focus on community engagement and buy-in, as well as policy relevance. In addition to such efforts, a project's sustainability can be further enhanced by diversifying the sources of financial support. Although this generates an additional burden in terms of project administration and coordination, it reduces the vulnerability of the project efforts to unexpected developments. Pursuing such goals will build trust across the field of practice, ensure that knowledge is mobilized to feed into practice and policy-making processes, and, in general, enhance the project's sustainability by promoting an atmosphere conducive to future action, cooperation and progress (122, 141).

With consideration of these generalized steps towards ensuring project sustainability, an agency survey can work from the beginning to lay the foundations for effective communication throughout the project cycle. As detailed in **SECTION 1.1**, a crucial first step should be the identification of relevant stakeholders through stakeholder mapping that encompasses not only the range of direct project beneficiaries, but also relevant actors across the research, practice, policy and donor spheres. The stakeholder mapping phase also provides a basis for sharing research outcomes as the project progresses, enabling synergy with other ongoing activities while avoiding the potential for overlapping or unnecessary duplication of effort.

The agency survey also provides a special opportunity for bridging the research–practice divide as well as community engagement and buy-in, because those participating in the survey are the stakeholders in the field themselves. They are in charge of setting the policies and implementing practical programmes aimed at child protection. The project's sustainability can be strengthened immediately through their participation in the survey, as they become more interested in the survey's results and potentially utilizing them for their own activities. This fact should be leveraged to further maximize policy and practical impact when setting up and conducting the study. Sending out early drafts of academic papers or policy responses to stakeholders for review has been shown to be successful (127).

Early involvement of stakeholders can lead to optimization of services and policies by presenting researchers with an opportunity to explain the benefits of using a child protection system based on scientific data, which can aid in identifying gaps in the system as well as regional disparities and underreporting. Understanding how the data will serve their own efforts not only helps to increase stakeholders' motivation to participate and hence increase the validity of data due to an increased participation rate, but also can have an overall ripple effect that raises awareness and spurs the use of more evidence-based practices in other child protection activities. By fostering deeper understanding of the benefits of an evidence-based approach, additional momentum is also formed for later take-up and use of the data generated in the study by the stakeholders working in this field.

One successful example of involving stakeholders at an early stage is the approach taken by the Together for Girls (www.togetherforgirls.org) initiative. Together for Girls aims to contribute to ending violence against children by conducting large, high-quality population surveys in different parts of the world. Surveys have been completed in several countries

Key considerations for project sustainability

■ **Communication:** crucial across all stages of a project, communication efforts must be tailored to match a range of different audiences to successfully generate understanding of the project's importance and feed its best practices and outcomes into policy-making and future activities.

■ **Monitoring and evaluation:** necessary for determining what aspects of the project are working well and which require further strengthening or alteration; repeated assessments can track change over time and add weight to outcomes.

■ **Policy relevance:** identifying the project's applicability and usefulness in a practical sense can contribute to bridging the research/policy divide, and ensure that best practices feed into policy-making.

■ **Stakeholder mapping:** identifying both direct beneficiaries of project activities as well as the broader stakeholder landscape is necessary for specifically tailoring project activities and for building collaborative efforts.

■ **Stakeholder engagement:** building on stakeholder mapping, efforts must be taken from the earliest possible stage to establish synergistic links with other stakeholders in order to ensure long-term project impact.

■ **Diversification of financial support:** building up a consortium of different funding bodies and/or collaborators can protect a project from unexpected shifts in availability of funding.

including Kenya, Swaziland, the United Republic of Tanzania and Zimbabwe. In each case, the respective government played an integral role from the outset of the project and disseminated the results on a national level. Following the surveys, efforts were undertaken to initiate evidence-based coordinated programme actions to address the issues identified in the surveys. This effective cooperation built trust and led to stakeholder buy-in that resulted in steps towards legal and policy reform, prevention of sexual violence, and improved services for children who have experienced sexual violence.

Once data collection activities for an agency survey have been concluded, it is essential to ensure that outcomes are communicated to stakeholders in a relevant and understandable manner. Summaries, policy briefs, presentations and infographics using a minimum of academic language can be prepared and targeted to match with key policy and practice concerns and trends. Careful and continuous communication efforts are needed to ensure that findings feed into policy processes and the evolving community of knowledge on child protection, thereby creating lasting impact. Furthermore, broadly disseminating the project's methodology and findings increases the number of professionals familiar with the project's approach, leading to greater sustainability in terms of human capacity.

One good example of successful dissemination of information to stakeholders is a large population-based assessment of 15- to 17-year-olds about victimization experiences in Switzerland, the Optimus Study (see www.optimusstudy.org). The survey was launched just in time to be included in national policy recommendations on necessary measures in the area of child and youth protection in 2012 (Postulat Fehr 07.3725). The results have also led to changes in practice that focus on establishing additional programmes to address peer-to peer sexual violence as a result of the finding that many cases involved perpetrators and victims in the same age group. Further, a group of key experts in the field have taken up the results and drafted recommendations based on the data. Finally, the findings have been included in teaching curricula at several institutions.

For agency surveys, repeated assessments constitute an important tool for further strengthening and building on initial results. The assessments are also a useful monitoring and evaluation instrument enabling an understanding of progress by countries and agencies towards responding to victimization. They allow for changes to be tracked over time, which makes it possible to determine whether newly introduced policies or practices do in fact lead to the desired change. Repeated assessments also provide an opportunity for incorporating continuous improvements into the methodology. One successful example is the British Crime Survey (142) in the United Kingdom. It was initially carried out in the 1970s on a local level (143), but the survey was repeated and improved over many years and finally taken up by the Home Office. Today, its purpose is to monitor national trends in reducing crime and people's perceptions of crime and the criminal justice system.

Ultimately, projects that incorporate strong stakeholder involvement, continuous and targeted communication activities and a sustained focus on policy applicability will be well-positioned to achieve sustainability. Such efforts will also ensure coherence and relevance, which will generate interest from philanthropic, bilateral or multilateral donors and further promote financial sustainability. Targeted communication with government stakeholders can also lead to elements of the project's approach or activities being translated directly into government policy. Among other things, this will require a comprehensive demonstration of a synergistic multi-stakeholder approach built on the best available data and coherent and policy-relevant project activities.

6. References

(1)   Finkelhor D, Ormrod R, Turner H, Hamby SL. The victimization of children and youth: a comprehensive, national survey. Child Maltreat. 2005; 10(1): 5–25. doi:10.1177/1077559504271287.

(2)   Häuser W, Schmutzer G, Brähler E, Glaesmer H. Misshandlungen in Kindheit und Jugend: Ergebnisse einer Umfrage in einer repräsentativen Stichprobe in der deutschen Bevölkerung [Maltreatment in childhood and adolescence: results from a survey of a representative sample of the German population]. 2011; Dtsch Arztebl Int. 108(17): 287–294. doi:10.3238/arztebl.2011.0287.

(3)   Lamers-Winkelman F, Slot NW, Bijl B, Vijbrief AC. Scholieren over mishandeling: resultaten van een landelijk onderzoek naar de omvang van kindermishandeling onder leerlingen van het voortgezet onderwijs [Asking pupils about abuse: The results of a national study on the prevalence of child abuse conducted in secondary education]. Duivendrecht: PI Research; 2007.

(4)   Jud A, Fluke J, Alink LR, Allan K, Fallon B, Kindler H et al. On the nature and scope of reported child maltreatment in high-income countries: opportunities for improving the evidence base. Paediatr Int Child Health. 2013; 33(4): 207–215. doi:10.1179/2046905513Y.0000000092.

(5)   Fallon B, Trocmé N, Fluke J, MacLaurin B, Tonmyr L, Yuan Y-Y. Methodological challenges in measuring child maltreatment. Child Abuse Negl. 2010; 34(1): 70–9.

(6)   Gilbert N. Combatting child abuse: international perspectives and trends. New York (NY): Oxford University Press; 1997.

(7)   National Center on Child Abuse and Neglect. Study findings: national incidence and severity of child abuse and neglect. Washington (DC): Department of Health and Human Services; 1981.

(8)   Sedlak AJ. National incidence and prevalence of child abuse and neglect. Washington (DC): Department of Health and Human Services; 1991.

(9)   Sedlak AJ, Broadhurst DD. Third National Incidence Study of Child Abuse and Neglect. Washington (DC): Department of Health and Human Services; 1996.

(10)   Sedlak AJ, Mettenburg J, Basena M, Petta I, McPherson K, Greene A et al. Fourth National Incidence Study of Child Abuse and Neglect (NIS-4): report to congress. Washington (DC): Department of Health and Human Services, Administration for Children and Families; 2010.

(11)   Public Health Agency of Canada (PHAC). Canadian Incidence Study of Reported Child Abuse and Neglect – 2008: Major Findings. Ottawa (ON): PHAC; 2010.

(12) Trocmé N, Fallon B, MacLaurin B, Daciuk J, Felstiner C, Black T et al. Canadian Incidence Study of Reported Child Abuse and Neglect 2003: Major Findings. Ottawa (ON): Minister of Public Works and Government Services Canada; 2005.

(13) Trocmé N, Fallon B, MacLaurin B, Sinha V, Black T, Fast E et al. Rates of maltreatment-related investigations in the CIS-1998, CIS-2003, and CIS-2008. In: Public Health Agency of Canada (PHAC), editors. Canadian Incidence Study of Reported Child Abuse and Neglect – 2008: Major Findings. Ottawa (ON): PHAC; 2010: 22–29.

(14) Trocmé N, MacLaurin BJ, Fallon BA, Daciuk JF, Tourigny M, Billingsley DA. Canadian Incidence Study of Reported Child Abuse and Neglect: Methodology. Can J Public Health. 2001; 92(4): 259–263.

(15) Fallon B, Trocmé N, MacLaurin B, Sinha V, Herbert A. Canadian Incidence Study of reported Child Abuse and Neglect – 2008: process evaluation report. Toronto (ON): University of Toronto; 2010.

(16) Euser EM, van IJzendoorn MH, Prinzie P, Bakermans-Kranenburg MJ. Prevalence of child maltreatment in the Netherlands. Child Maltreat. 2010; 15(1): 5–17. doi:10.1177/1077559509345904.

(17) Euser S, Alink LR, Pannebakker F, Vogels T, Bakermans-Kranenburg MJ, van IJzendoorn MH. The prevalence of child maltreatment in the Netherlands across a 5-year period. Child Abuse Negl. 2013; 37(10): 841–851. doi: 10.1016/j.chiabu.2013.07.004.

(18) Averdijk M, Müller-Johnson K, Eisner M. Sexual victimization of children and adolescents in Switzerland: final report for the UBS Optimus Foundation. Zürich: UBS Optimus Foundation; 2011.

(19) Szabo-Lael R, Hasin T. At-risk children and youth: results of the identification and mapping conducted by the national program for children and youth at risk. Jerusalem: Myers-JDC-Brookdale Institute; 2011.

(20) Ntinapogias A, Nikolaidis G. Case-based surveillance study: Balkan report (on the basis of national reports prepared by BECAN WP4 partners). Athens: Institute of Child Health, Department of Mental Health & Social Welfare; 2013.

(21) Ben-Arieh A, Haj-Yahia MM. The "geography" of child maltreatment in Israel: findings from a national data set of cases reported to the social services. Child Abuse Negl. 2006; 30(9): 991–1003. doi:10.1016/j.chiabu.2006.02.014.

(22) Department of Health and Human Services. Child maltreatment 1995. Washington (DC): U.S. Government Printing Office; 1997.

(23) Department of Health and Human Services. Child Maltreatment 2006. Washington (DC): U.S. Government Printing Office; 2008.

(24) Department of Health and Human Services (2013). Child Maltreatment 2012. Washington, (DC): Author.

(25) Mansell J. Stabilisation of the statutory child protection response: managing to a specified level of risk assurance. Soc Policy J N. Z. 2006; 28: 77–93.

(26) Mansell J. The underlying instability in statutory child protection: understanding the system dynamics driving risk assurance levels. Soc Policy J N. Z. 2006; 28: 97–132.

(27) Pai KS, Kim SY, Chung YK, Ryu KH. The present state of child abuse in Korea and its system for child protection. Korean J Pediatr. 2009; 52(11): 1185–1193. doi:10.3345/kjp.2009.52.11.1185.

(28) Al Eissa M, Almuneef M. Child abuse and neglect in Saudi Arabia: journey of recognition to implementation of national prevention strategies. Child Abuse Negl. 2010; 34(1): 28–33. doi:10.1016/j.chiabu.2009.08.011.

(29) Department of Education. Characteristics of children in need in England, 2012–2013. London: Author; 2013.

(30) The Scottish Government. Children's social work statistics Scotland, 2012–13. Edinburgh: Author; 2014.

(31) Munro ER, Brown R, Manful E. Safeguarding children statistics: the availability and comparability of data in the UK. London: Department of Education; 2011.

(32) Australian Institute of Health and Welfare. A new approach to national child protection data: implementation of the child protection national minimum data set. Canberra: Author; 2014.

(33) Kind en Gezin. The child in Flanders. Brussel: Author; 2011 (http://www.kindengezin.be/algemeen/english-pages.jsp, accessed 13 October 2014).

(34) Konferenz der Kantone für Kindes- und Erwachsenenschutz (KOKES). Schweizerische Statistik Kindesschutzmassnahmen: Jahresvergleich 2001–2010 [Swiss statistics of child protection orders: Comparison between 2001 and 2010]. Z Kindes-Erwachsenenschutz. 2011; 66(5): 423.

(35) Sedlak AJ, Mettenburg J, Winglee M, Ciarico J, Basena, Rust K et al. Fourth National Incidence Study of Child Abuse and Neglect (NIS-4) Technical Report III: Analysis Report [Prepared under contract to the U.S. Department of Health and Human Services] Rockville (MD): Westat, Inc; 2010.

(36) Sinha V, Trocmé N, Fallon B, MacLaurin B, Fast E, Prokop S et al. Kiskisik awasisak: remember the children: understanding the overrepresentation of first nations children in the child welfare system. Ontario: Assembly of First Nations; 2011 (http://cwrp.ca/publications/2280, accessed 17 November 2014).

(37) Gilbert R, Fluke J, O'Donnell M, Gonzalez-Izquierdo A, Brownell M, Gulliver P et al. Child maltreatment: variation in trends and policies in six developed countries. Lancet. 2012; 379(9817): 758–772. doi:10.1016/S0140-6736(11)61087-8.

(38) Gilbert R, Kemp A, Thoburn J, Sidebotham P, Radford L, Glaser D et al. Child maltreatment 2: recognising and responding to child maltreatment. Lancet. 2009; 373(9658): 167–180. doi:10.1016/S0140-6736(08)61707-9.

(39) Trocmé N, Fallon B, MacLaurin B, Sinha V, Black T, Fast E et al. Canadian Incidence Study of Reported Child Abuse and Neglect – 2008: Executive Summary & Chapters 1–5. Ottawa (ON): Public Health Agency of Canada; 2010.

(40) Kyte A, Trocmé N, Chamberland C. Evaluating where we're at with differential response. Child Abuse Negl. 2013; 37(2–3): 125–132. doi:10.1016/j.chiabu.2012.10.003.

(41) Finkelhor D, Lannen P, Quayle E. Optimus Study: a cross-national research initiative on protecting children and youth [synthesis]. Zürich: UBS Optimus Foundation; 2011.

(42) Mikton C. Technical report on the assessment of readiness to implement evidence-based child maltreatment prevention programmes of Brazil, the Former Yoguslav Republic of Macedonia, Malaysia, Saudi Arabia, and South Africa. Geneva: World Health Organization; 2012.

(43) Mikton C, Mehra R, Butchart A, Addiss D, Almuneef M, Cardia N et al. A multidimensional model for child maltreatment prevention readiness in low- and middle-income countries. J Community Psychol. 2011; 39(7): 826–843. doi: 10.1002/Jcop.20474.

(44) Wulczyn F, Daro D, Fluke J, Feldman S, Glodek C, Lifanda K. Adapting a systems approach to child protection: key concepts and considerations. New York (NY): United Nations Children's Fund (UNICEF); 2010.

(45) Department of Health and Human Services. Child Maltreatment 2010. Washington, (DC): Author; 2011.

(46) Eckenrode J, Dineen M. Child maltreatment declines 12% 2006–2007. Child-Maltreatment-Research-L (CMRL). Ithaca (NY): National Data Archive on Child Abuse and Neglect; 2009 (http://www.ndacan.cornell.edu/NDACAN/CMRLListserv.html, accessed 15 October 2009).

(47) Laumann EO, Michael RT, Gagnon JH. A political history of the national sex survey of adults. Fam Plann Perspect. 1994; 26(1): 34–38.

(48) Zell ER, Ezzati-Rice TM, Battaglia MP, Wright RA. National Immunization Survey: the methodology of a vaccination surveillance system. Public Health Rep. 2000; 115(1): 65–77.

(49) Hélie S, Turcotte D, Trocmé N, Tourigny M. Étude d'incidence québécoise sur les situations évaluées en protection de la jeunesse en 2008 (ÉIQ-2008): rapport final. Montréal: Centre jeunesse de Montréal-Institut universitaire; 2012.

(50) Jud A, Lips U, Landolt MA. Characteristics associated with maltreatment types in children referred to a hospital protection team. Eur J Pediatr. 2010; 169(2): 173–180. doi:10.1007/s00431-009-1001-5.

(51) Trocmé N, Fallon B, MacLaurin B, Sinha V, Black T, Fast E et al. Methodology. In: Public Health Agency of Canada (PHAC), editors. Canadian Incidence Study of Reported Child Abuse and Neglect – 2008: Major Findings. Ottawa (ON): PHAC; 2010: pp. 12–21.

(52) Centers for Disease Control and Prevention. HIV surveillance-United States, 1981–2008. MMWR Morb Mortal Wkly Rep. 2011; 60(21): 689–693.

(53) Haar K, Bremer V, Houareau C, Meyer T, Desai S, Thamm M et al. Risk factors for chlamydia trachomatis infection in adolescents: results from a representative population-based survey in Germany, 2003–2006. 2013; Euro Surveill. 18(34) (http://www.eurosurveillance.org/ViewArticle.aspx?ArticleId=20562, accessed 17 November 2014).

(54) Ivankovich MB, Leichliter JS, Douglas JM Jr. Measurement of sexual health in the U.S.: an inventory of nationally representative surveys and surveillance systems. Public Health Rep. 2013; 128 Suppl 1: 62–72.

(55)   Reece M, Herbenick D, Schick V, Sanders SA, Dodge B, Fortenberry JD. Background and considerations on the National Survey of Sexual Health and Behavior (NSSHB) from the investigators. J Sex Med. 2010; 7 Suppl 5: 243–245. doi:10.1111/j.1743-6109.2010.02038.x.

(56)   Maier T, Mohler-Kuo M, Landolt MA, Schnyder U, Jud A. The tip of the iceberg. Incidence of disclosed cases of child sexual abuse in Switzerland: results from a nationwide agency survey. Int J Public Health. 2013; 58: 875–883. doi:10.1007/s00038-013-0498-6.

(57)   Simon P. Collecting ethnic statistics in Europe: a review. Ethn Racial Stud. 2012; 35(8): 1366–1391. doi:10.1080/01419870.2011.607507.

(58)   Cross TP, Walsh WA, Simone M, Jones LM. Prosecution of child abuse: a meta-analysis of rates of criminal justice decisions. Trauma Violence Abuse. 2003; 4(4): 323–340. doi:10.1177/1524838003256561.

(59)   Wolak J, Mitchell KJ, Finkelhor D. Methodology report: 3rd National Juvenile Online Victimization (NJOV3) Study. Durham (NH): Crimes Against Children Research Center (CCRC); 2011.

(60)   Sedlak AJ, Webb MB. 4th National incidence study of child abuse and neglect – project summary. Rockville (MD): Westat; 2008.

(61)   Fallon B, Trocmé N, MacLaurin B, Sinha V, Hélie S, Turcotte D et al. Canadian Incidence Study of reported Child Abuse and Neglect 2008 (CIS-2008): study methods. Montreal (QC): McGill Centre for Research on Children and Families; 2013.

(62)   Gaskell GD, Wright DB, O'Muircheartaigh CA. Telescoping of landmark events – implications for survey research. Public Opin Q. 2000; 64(1): 77–89. doi:10.1086/316761.

(63)   Daniel J. Sampling essentials: practical guidelines for making sampling choices. Thousand Oaks (CA): Sage Publications; 2011.

(64)   Levy PS, Lemeshow S. Sampling of populations methods and applications. 4th ed. New York (NY): Wiley; 2013.

(65)   Lohr SL. Sampling: design and analysis. 2nd ed. Boston: BROOKS/COLE Cengage Learning Emea; 2010.

(66)   Delgado-Rodríguez M, Llorca J. Bias. J Epidemiol Community Health. 2004; 58(8): 635–641. doi:10.1136/jech.2003.008466.

(67)   Department of Health and Human Services. Child Maltreatment 2011. Washington (DC): Author; 2012.

(68)   Alink LRA, van IJzendoorn M, Bakermans-Kranenburg M, Pannebakker F, Vogels T, Euser S. Kindermishandeling in Nederland anno 2010: de tweede nationale prevalentiestudie mishandeling van kinderen en jeugdigen (NPM-2010) [The second Netherlands' prevalence study of maltreatment of children and youth (NPM-2010)]. Leiden: Casimir; 2011.

(69)   Leeb RT, Paulozzi L, Melanson C, Simon T, Arias I. Child maltreatment surveillance: uniform definitions for public health and recommended data elements, version 1.0. Atlanta (GA): Centers for Disease Control and Prevention, National Center for Injury Prevention and Control; 2008.

(70) United Nations. Convention on the rights of the child. New York: Author; 1989.

(71) Rothwell DW, de Boer KR. Measuring economic hardship in child maltreatment research: evidence from Canada. Child Indic Res. 2014; 7(2): 301–320. doi:10.1007/s12187-013-9222-6.

(72) Simon P. Statistics, french social sciences and ethnic and racial social relations. Rev fr social. 2010; 51(1): 159–174.

(73) Jud A, Fallon B, Trocmé N. Who gets services and who does not? Multi-level approach to the decision for ongoing child welfare or referral to specialized services. Child Youth Serv Rev. 2012; 34(5): 983–988. doi: 10.1016/j.childyouth.2012.01.030.

(74) Baumann DJ, Dalgleish, L, Fluke J, Kern H. The Decision-Making Ecology. Washington (DC): American Humane Association; 2011.

(75) Chabot M, Fallon B, Tonmyr L, MacLaurin B, Fluke J, Blackstock C. Exploring alternate specifications to explain agency-level effects in placement decisions regarding aboriginal children: further analysis of the Canadian Incidence Study of Reported Child Abuse and Neglect Part B. Child Abuse Negl. 2013; 37(1): 61–76. doi:10.1016/j.chiabu.2012.10.002.

(76) Fallon B, Chabot M, Fluke J, Blackstock C, MacLaurin B, Tonmyr L. Placement decisions and disparities among Aboriginal children: further analysis of the Canadian Incidence Study of reported Child Abuse and Neglect part A: comparisons of the 1998 and 2003 surveys. Child Abuse Negl. 2013; 37(1): 47–60. doi:10.1016/j.chiabu.2012.10.001.

(77) Wulczyn F, Chen L, Courtney M. Family reunification in a social structural context. Child Youth Serv Rev. 2011: 33(3): 424–430. doi:10.1016/j.childyouth.2010.06.021.

(78) Cicchetti D, Toth SL. Child maltreatment. Annu Rev Clin Psychol. 2005; 1: 409–438. doi:10.1146/annurev.clinpsy.1.102803.144029.

(79) Herrenkohl RC. The definition of child maltreatment: from case study to construct. Child Abuse Negl. 2005; 29(5): 413–424. doi:10.1016/j.chiabu.2005.04.002.

(80) English DJ, Graham JC, Litrownik AJ, Everson M, Bangdiwala SI. Defining maltreatment chronicity: are there differences in child outcomes? Child Abuse Negl. 2005; 29(5): 575–595.

(81) Tyler S, Allison K, Winsler A. Child neglect: developmental consequences, intervention, and policy implications. Child Youth Care Forum. 2006; 35(1): 1–20.

(82) English DJ, the LONGSCAN Investigators. Modified Maltreatment Classification System (MMCS). Chapel Hill (NC): LONGSCAN consortium; 1997 (http://www.iprc.unc.edu/longscan/, accessed 13 June 2014).

(83) Trocmé N. Epidemiology of child maltreatment. In: Lindsey D, Shlonsky A, editors. Child welfare research: advances for practice and policy. New York (NY): Oxford University Press; 2008: 15–24.

(84) Fallon B, Trocmé N, Maclaurin B. Should child protection services respond differently to maltreatment, risk of maltreatment, and risk of harm?. Child Abuse Negl. 2011; 35(4): 236–239. doi:S0145-2134(11)00069-X.

(85) Hindley N, Ramchandani PG, Jones DP. Risk factors for recurrence of maltreatment: a systematic review. Arch Dis Child. 2006; 91(9): 744–752. doi:10.1136/adc.2005.085639.

(86) Litrownik AJ, Lau A, English DJ, Briggs E, Newton RR, Romney S et al. Measuring the severity of child maltreatment. Child Abuse Negl. 2005; 29(5): 553–573. doi:10.1016/j.chiabu.2003.08.010.

(87) Hildyard KL, Wolfe DA. Child neglect: developmental issues and outcomes. Child Abuse Negl. 2002; 26(6–7): 679–695. doi:10.1016/S0145-2134(02)00341-1.

(88) Lansford JE, Dodge KA, Pettit GS, Bates JE, Crozier J, Kaplow J. A 12-year prospective study of the long-term effects of early child physical maltreatment on psychological, behavioral, and academic problems in adolescence. Arch Pediatr Adolesc Med. 2002; 156(8): 824–830. doi:poa20065.

(89) Paolucci EO, Genuis ML, Violato C. A meta-analysis of the published research on the effects of child sexual abuse. J Psychol. 2001; 135(1): 17–36. doi:10.1080/00223980109603677.

(90) Springer KW, Sheridan J, Kuo D, Carnes M. The long-term health outcomes of childhood abuse. An overview and a call to action. J Gen Intern Med. 2003; 18(10): 864–870.

(91) Black DA, Heyman, RE, & Smith Slep AM. Risk factors for child sexual abuse. Aggress Violent Behav. 2001; 6(2–3): 203–229. doi:10.1016/S1359-1789(00)00023-9.

(92) Bouvier P, Halperin D, Rey H, Jaffe PD, Laederach J, Mounoud RL et al. Typology and correlates of sexual abuse in children and youth: multivariate analyses in a prevalence study in Geneva. Child Abuse Negl. 1999; 23(8): 779–790. doi: S0145-2134(99)00050-2.

(93) McSherry D. Understanding and addressing the "neglect of neglect": Why are we making a mole-hill out of a mountain? Child Abuse Negl. 2007; 31(6): 607–614. doi:10.1016/j.chiabu.2006.08.011.

(94) Heyman RE, Smith Slep AM. Risk factors for family violence: introduction to the special series. Aggress Violent Behav. 2001; 6(2–3): 115–119. doi:10.1016/S1359-1789(00)00020-3.

(95) Schumacher JA, Smith Slep AM, Heyman RE. Risk factors for child neglect. Aggress Violent Behav. 2001; 6(2–3): 231–254. doi:10.1016/S1359-1789(00)00024-0.

(96) Black, DA, Smith Slep AM, Heyman RE. Risk factors for child psychological abuse. Aggress Violent Behav. 2001; 6(2–3): 189–201. doi:10.1016/S1359-1789(00)00022-7.

(97) Black DA, Heyman RE, Smith Slep AM. Risk factors for child physical abuse. Aggress Violent Behav. 2001; 6(2–3): 121–188. doi:10.1016/S1359-1789(00)00021-5.

(98) Kline RB. Principles and practice of structural equation modeling. 2nd ed. New York: The Guilford Press; 2005.

(99) Browne RP, McNicholas PD. Mixture and Latent Class Models in Longitudinal and Other Settings. In: Scott MA, Simonoff JS, Marx BD, editors. The SAGE handbook of multilevel modeling. London: Sage; 2013: 357–370.

(100) Bartholomew DJ, Steele F, Moustakr I, Galbraith JI. Analysis of multivariate social science data. 2nd ed. Boca Raton: CRC Press; 2008.

(101) Abner KS. Dimensions of structural disadvantage: a latent class analysis of a neighborhood measure in child welfare data. 2014; J Soc Serv Res. 40(1): 121–134. doi: 10.1080/01488376.2013.852651.

(102) Guo S, Fraser MW. Propensity score analysis statistical methods and applications. Los Angeles: SAGE; 2010.

(103) McCutcheon AL. Basic concepts and procedures in single- and multiple-group latent class analysis. In: Hagenaars JA, McCutcheon AL, editors. Applied latent class analysis. Cambridge: Cambridge University Press; 2002: 56–85.

(104) Hibberts M, Johnson RB, Hudson K. Common survey sampling techniques. In: Gideon L, editor. Handbook of survey methodology for the social sciences. New York (NY): Springer; 2012: 53–74.

(105) Dumais J, Gough JH. Computing estimates and their sampling errors from complex samples. In: Greaney V, Kellaghan T, editors. Implementing a national assessment of educational achievement. Washington (DC): The World Bank; 2005: 215 – 223.

(106) Lepkowski J, Bowles J. Sampling error software for personal computers. Surv Stat. 1996; 35: 10–17.

(107) Gill J, Womack AJ. The multilevel model framework. In: Scott MA, Simonoff JS, Marx BD, editors. The SAGE handbook of multilevel modeling. London: SAGE; 2013: 2–20.

(108) Snijders, TAB, Bosker RJ. Multilevel analysis an introduction to basic and advanced multilevel modelling. 2nd ed. London: SAGE; 2012.

(109) Bauer DJ. Estimating multilevel linear models as structural equation models. J Educ Behav Statistics. 2003; 28(2): 135–167.

(110) Dubowitz H, Kim J, Black MM, Weisbart C, Semiatin J, Magder LS. Identifying children at high risk for a child maltreatment report. Child Abuse Negl. 2011; 35(2): 96–104. doi: S0145-2134(11)00013-5.

(111) Snijders TAB, Berkhof J. Diagnostic checks for multilevel models. In: Leeuw JD, Meijer E, editors. Handbook of multilevel analysis. New York (NY): Springer; 2008: 141–176.

(112) Merlo J, Chaix B, Ohlsson H, Beckman A, Johnell K, Hjerpe P. A brief conceptual tutorial of multilevel analysis in social epidemiology: using measures of clustering in multilevel logistic regression to investigate contextual phenomena. J Epidemiol Community Health. 2006; 60(4): 290–297.

(113) Tarling R. Statistical modelling for social researchers: principles and practice. London: Routledge; 2009.

(114) Albert VN. Using time-series analysis to evaluate the impact of policy initiatives in child welfare. Eval Program Plan. 2001; 24(2): 109–117. doi:10.1016/S0149-7189(01)00002-7.

(115) Esposito T, Trocmé N, Chabot M, Shlonsky A, Collin-Vézina D, Sinha V. Placement of children in out-of-home care in Québec. Canada: When and for whom initial out-of-home placement is most likely to occur. Child Youth Serv Rev. 2013; 35(12): 2031–2039.

(116)   Farmer EMZ, Mustillo S, Burns BJ, Holden EW. Use and predictors of out-of-home placements within systems of care. J Emot Behav Disord. 2008; 16(1): 5–14. doi:10.1177/1063426607310845.

(117)   Wulczyn F, Chen L. Placement stability and movement trajectories. In: Fernandez E, Barth RP, editors. How does foster care work? International evidence on outcomes. London: Jessica Kingsley Publishers; 2010: 65–80.

(118)   Wooldridge JM. Introductory econometrics: a modern approach. 5th international ed. Andover: South-Western; 2013.

(119)   Box-Steffensmeier JM, Jones BS. Event history modeling: a guide for social scientists. Cambridge: University Press; 2004.

(120)   Cooper A, Levin, B, Campbell C. The growing (but still limited) importance of evidence in education policy and practice. J Educ Change. 2009; 10: 159–171.

(121)   Trocmé N, Esposito T, Laurendeau C, Thomson W, Milne L. La mobilisation des connaissances en protection de l'enfance. Criminol. 2009; 42(1): 33–59. doi:10.7202/029807ar.

(122)   Lomas J. Using 'linkage and exchange' to move research into policy at a Canadian foundation. Health Aff (Millwood). 2000; 19(3): 236–240. doi: 10.1377/hlthaff.19.3.236.

(123)   Crosnoe R. Opportunities for and challenges of translating educational and developmental research into policy and intervention. In: Wethington E, Dunifon RE, editors. Research for the public good: applying the methods of translational research to improve human health and well-being. Washington (DC): American Psychological Association; 2012: 53–72.

(124)   Graham ID, Logan J, Harrison MB, Straus SE, Tetroe J, Caswell W et al. Lost in knowledge translation: time for a map? J Contin Educ Health Prof. 2006; 26(1): 13–24. doi:10.1002/chp.47.

(125)   Feldman S. Strangers in the night: research and managed mental health care. Health Aff (Millwood). 1999; 18(5): 48–51.

(126)   Williams-Mbengue N, Ramirez-Fry K, Crane K. Differential response approach in child protective services: an analysis of state legislative provisions. Washington (DC): National Conference of State Legislatures; 2010.

(127)   Fallon B, Trocmé N, MacLaurin B, Knoke D, Black T, Felstiner C. Supporting secondary analyses of the Canadian Incidence Studies of reported Child Abuse and Neglect (CIS). In: Léveillé S, Trocmé N, Brown I, Chamberland C, editors. Research-community partnership in child welfare. Toronto (ON): Centre of Excellence for Child Welfare; 2011.

(128)   Pedrini S, Bachtiger A, Steenbergen MR. Deliberative inclusion of minorities: patterns of reciprocity among linguistic groups in Switzerland. Eur Political Sci Rev. 2013; 5(3): 483–512. doi:10.1017/S1755773912000239.

(129)   Trocmé N, Fallon B, MacLaurin B, Sinha V, Black T, Fast E et al. Chapter 1: introduction. In: Public Health Agency of Canada (PHAC), editors. Canadian Incidence Study of Reported Child Abuse and Neglect – 2008: Major Findings. Ottawa (ON): PHAC; 2010: 7–11.

(130) Spencer V. Language, history and the nation: an historical approach to evaluating language and cultural claims. Nations Natl. 2008; 14(2): 241–259. doi:10.1111/j.1469-8129.2008.00334.x.

(131) Tham P, Meagher G. Working in human services: how do experiences and working conditions in child welfare social work compare? Br J Soc Work. 2009; 39: 807–827. doi:10.1093/bjsw/bcm170.

(132) Yamatani H, Engel R, Spjeldnes S. Child welfare worker caseload: what's just right? Soc Work. 2009; 54(4): 361–368. doi:10.1093/sw/54.4.361.

(133) Council on Accreditation (COA). Child protective services (CA CPS): CA CPS 14 – personnel. New York (NY): Author; 2014 (http://coanet.org/standard/ca-cps/14/, accessed 25 April 2014).

(134) Institute of Medicine, National Research Council. New directions in child abuse and neglect research. Washington, DC: The National Academies Press; 2014.

(135) Van IJzendoorn MH, Prinzie PJ, Euser EM, Groeneveld MG, Brilleslijper-Kater SN, Van Noort-Van der Linden AMT et al. Kindermishandeling in Nederland anno 2005: de nationale prevalentiestudie mishandeling van kinderen en jeugdigen (NPM-2005) [The Netherlands' prevalence study of maltreatment of children and youth (NPM-2005)]. Leiden: Casimir Publishers; 2007.

(136) McCormack L, Sheridan S, Lewis M, Boudewyns V, Melvin CL, Kistler C et al. Communication and dissemination strategies to facilitate the use of health-related evidence (Evidence Report/Technology Assessment No. 213). Rockville (MD): RTI International–University of North Carolina Evidence-based Practice Center; 2013.

(137) Rabin BA, Brownson RC, Haire-Joshu D, Kreuter MW, Weaver NL. A glossary for dissemination and implementation research in health. J Public Health Manag Pract. 2008; 14(2): 117–123. doi:10.1097/01.PHH.0000311888.06252.bb.

(138) Gagnon ML. Moving knowledge to action through dissemination and exchange. J Clin Epidemiol. 2011; 64(1): 25–31. doi:10.1016/j.jclinepi.2009.08.013.

(139) Reardon R, Lavis J, Gibson J. From research to practice: a knowledge transfer planning guide. Toronto (ON): Institute of Work and Health; 2006.

(140) European Commission. Handbook of sustainability – sustainability of international cooperation projects in the field of higher education and vocational training. Luxemburg: Office for Official Publications of the European Communities; 2006.

(141) Bennet G, Jessani N. The knowledge translation toolkit bridging the know-do gap: a resource for researchers. Ottawa (ON): International Development Research Centre; 2011.

(142) Walker A, Kershaw C, Nicholas S. Crime in England and Wales 2005/06 [Home Office Statistical Bulletin 12/06]. London: Home Office; 2006.

(143) Sparks R, Genn H, Dodd D. Surveying victims. Chichester: John Wiley; 1977.